"Nancy Head's *Restoring the Shattered* leads the reader through a compelling and emotional story of the life of a woman who has experienced the best and worst moments of the modern-day church. At the same time, Nancy artfully weaves the surprisingly fascinating history of the church's theology and its politics in a way that will challenge all of us to walk worthy of our calling."

—BOB GRESH,
husband of best-selling author Dannah Gresh
(nearly half a million books sold)

"In *Restoring the Shattered*, Nancy's account of her life experience, intertwined with historic events and lessons from faith leaders of many disciplines, mirrors the personal problems and societal tensions present in the Christian church. Ironically, as the Reverend Billy Graham came to Altoona in 1949 and found discourse in the church strained enough to test his commitment to evangelism, Nancy sees the same discourse today stretching well beyond the city limits of her hometown. Fortunately, through faith and determination, the difficult times strengthened Billy's and Nancy's resolve and both were better equipped to encourage others in their journey with Christ."

T0163765

–JOHN H. EICHELBERGER, JR.,
Pennsylvania State Senator

"I'm a pastor who Nancy gets to hear all the time. It's been a joy and a privilege to read her and hear what she has to say. She is the real deal! Her passion and insight come through in everything she does, including in her book *Restoring the Shattered*. This is a joy to read, and it can help you on your life's journey."

—REVEREND JOHN COLLINS,
First Church of Christ, Altoona, Pennsylvania

"Since the beginning of Christendom, believers have not only engaged in the discussion of difference versus agreement on the doctrines we find within the Bible but have often found themselves participating in the nature of disagreement that brings hurt to individuals and to the church. In her book *Restoring the Shattered*, Nancy sensitively traces the history of division and encourages the church to focus on those doctrines that bring both harmony and light. She does this through sharing her struggles of separation within her own family and uses the images of shattered glass to illustrate our brokenness. It is a subject that we should not neglect and one that will benefit the church and individuals."

—STELLA PRICE,
author of *Chosen for Choson* (Korea) and *God's Collaborator*

"When I met Nancy, she served a university-appointed role as a mentor-teacher to me. She gave every impression of a whole person, a great look for a mentor to have. But like all of us, the external appearance of perfection exists only on the surface. Yet Nancy does have an internal assurance of completion—one which comes from our Savior, Jesus Christ. *Restoring the Shattered* offers readers a chance to examine breaks on every layer to see the combined work of restoration on which Nancy and Christ have embarked and offers hope and advice for those who wish to traverse that same path with him."

—REVEREND ADAM SHELLENBARGER,
pastor, Joppatown Christian Church, Joppatown, Maryland

"*Restoring the Shattered* is a wonderful first-person perspective of a person on the path of Christianity. It shows the commonality of Christian beliefs that can be shared in our confusing world."

—GEORGE FOSTER,
businessman and lay Catholic

Restoring THE SHATTERED

Restoring
THE SHATTERED

Illustrating Christ's Love
Through the Church in One Accord

NANCY E. HEAD

NASHVILLE

NEW YORK • LONDON • MELBOURNE • VANCOUVER

RESTORING THE SHATTERED

© 2019 Nancy E. Head

Published in New York, New York, by Morgan James Publishing.
Morgan James is a trademark of Morgan James, LLC.
www.MorganJamesPublishing.com

The Morgan James Speakers Group can bring authors to your live event.
For more information or to book an event visit The Morgan James Speakers Group at
www.TheMorganJamesSpeakersGroup.com.

ISBN 978-1-64279-049-8 paperback
ISBN 978-1-64279-050-4 eBook
Library of Congress Control Number: 2018939796

Cover & Interior Design by:
Megan Whitney Dillon
Creative Ninja Designs
megan@creativeninjadesigns.com

In an effort to support local communities, raise awareness and funds, Morgan James
Publishing donates a percentage of all book sales for the life of each book to
Habitat for Humanity Peninsula and Greater Williamsburg.

Get involved today! Visit
www.MorganJamesBuilds.com

For shattered hearts in need of the Master's holy touch

Contents

Foreword

Nancy Head and I are family. Consider.

We are members of the same race—the human race—though our ethnicities may differ.

We are both natural born American citizens, we have traveled to other countries, and we each have an abiding interest in what happens in the world.

Both of us have experienced marriage and divorce. We entered marriage with our spouses, hoping it would last a lifetime, but that was not to be. And we both found new marital life with other partners and built new lives on better foundations.

Both of us have children, now adults, whom we have always loved and always will.

And both of us are broken people but not shattered. We have certainly felt as if our lives were falling apart and could have become ruins. But what ultimately restored us both in our individual and family lives was not possessions, money, government assistance, or any other merely human contrivance. In fact, what restored us is not a what at all but a who. And not just one who but a community of whos. The triune God of Father, Son, and Holy Spirit worked in us to restore and renew us. And this same God worked through his community of believers called the church to help accomplish this healing work. All of these whos—these persons—made what seemed nearly impossible in our lives become an incredible reality.

In this restoration work, Nancy and I also received God's grace and healing through believers from more than one Christian tradition. We witnessed and received all kinds of help from fellow evangelical Protestants as well as from Roman Catholics and Orthodox Christians. Prayers, job assistance, listening ears, useful counsel, groceries, financial gifts, theological and biblical insights, and a host of other forms of help came from Christ's full church community.

We are also among a growing number of Christ-followers who desire Christians from all three Christian traditions to work together, engage the culture together, minister together, worship together, petition God together, and rise up and praise him together for the amazing work he has done, continues to do, and will do forevermore. We do not see this as a minimalist ecumenism—a unity built on denying our differences while giving mere lip service to our commonalities. Not at all. Instead, Nancy and I firmly believe—and can demonstrate—that what all Christians have in common doctrinally, historically, and practically far outweighs what differentiates us. We realize that not all Christians share our ecumenical outlook on the church, but we see this more as fallout from misunderstandings and even distortions that keep getting passed along no matter how many times they have been addressed—and usually addressed well.

I fully grant that some of what differentiates one tradition from another and even various churches within each of those traditions needs to be discussed, rigorously and robustly even. But in the end, we Christians should depart as friends, not as enemies, as fellow family members, not as alienated hostiles. The Lord Jesus we all share as fellow Christians prayed to the Father, that all those who believed in him "may all be one; even as You, Father, are in Me and I in You, that they also may be in Us, so that the world may believe that You sent Me." Jesus then asked the Father that all his followers "may be perfected in unity, so that the world may know that You sent Me, and loved them, even as You have loved Me" (John 17:21, 23). Family members don't have to agree with one another on everything, but they should exhibit toward one another the love of the Lover who saved them and who "desires all men to be saved and to come to the knowledge of the truth" (1 Timothy 2:4).

All of these commonalities I have with Nancy drew me to her book, *Restoring the Shattered*. But the differences in her approach to the ecumenical spirit drew me in even more. Nancy opens up on these pages. She shares her life and uses it as a window through which to understand what the church has experienced over the centuries: the triumphs and the losses, the joys and the pains, acceptance and rejection, shared outlooks and broken trust, creeds that bind and creeds that divide. Nancy sees parallels between her personal and family life and the life of the church. And just as she has experienced divine grace, forgiveness, and aid in so many forms, so she shares how the church collectively, institutionally, and even individually in and through its members has received divine favor, sometimes in spite of itself.

Another striking difference Nancy brings to the ecumenical discussion is the imagery of glass. Glass lets us see into a room as well as out of it. Glass allows light in and can allow it to be beamed out. Colored glass can color what we see through it, and stained glass can open to us vistas of art, beauty, and story. But glass can also scratch, crack, break into chunks, and even shatter. Glass can become dingy, cutting down, even blocking the light that seeks to shine through it. Nancy compares the church and us as its members to glass. When we are at our best, the Light that is Christ robustly shines through us and our assemblies into a dark, often oppressive world, conveying to it truth, hope, redemption, forgiveness, and new life. But when our lives are marred and broken, like cracked or even shattered glass, the Light can still come through, but often it appears fragmented and diminished. Of course, Christ has more means than just us through whom to shine his light. And he has always done some of his best work in human history through lives that seem to have come to a ruinous end. Nancy brings out all of these nuances and more through the analogy of glass.

Along with all the imagery and issues Nancy writes about, what beams through brightest is the personal—the personal side of being human, married, a family member, a Christ-follower, and a recipient and servant in a local and worldwide church. Indeed, what I found often in Nancy's pages is myself. Parts of my history, my family's history, my life in Christ's church, and my private walk with him, all shining through Nancy's journey. I imagine that you too will find aspects of your life embedded here.

At many points as I read, I found myself nodding in agreement with Nancy. Her life story, though not mine in many of its details, resonates with mine in more ways than I can share here. We have more in common in our earthly journey than differences, though the differences matter. I also found myself concurring with most of her assessments of church history and Christian behavior over the centuries. While I differ with her on some details, the overall thrust of her message and the case she makes getting there are more than worthy of our consideration as brothers and sisters in Christ.

I will not presume on how you will respond to what Nancy says here. All I ask is that you give her a fair-minded hearing. Listen. Reflect. Discuss this book with others. Pray about her counsel. She comes to you—to all of us who have entered into God's family through Jesus Christ—and asks that you will consider the need for and way to a renewed Christian accord. I have long embraced this vision. And through *Restoring the Shattered*, I hope many more within the family will make this vision their own too.

We live in a broken and divided world—a world separated by opposing political parties and philosophies, by conflicting worldviews (some religious and others irreligious), by distrust among various ethnic groups, by competing moralities and immoralities, and on the list goes. Litigation, legislation, a police force, armies, shaming, manipulation, language control, group-think, and a host of other human-centered approaches will not unite our damaged world. Even the church, with all of its resources, cannot achieve such a task; only our Lord can and will one day do that.

But what we, the church, can do is show the world a better way to live. A life path of genuine comm-unity. A life of mutual sharing and support. A family life that desires for its members an individuality of giftedness, service, thought, vocation, loves, and friendships while encouraging communal unity in doctrinal essentials, love for one another, and growth toward spiritual maturity.

Life can be different.

Life can be better.

Life can bring more life.

The church—Orthodox, Catholic, and Protestant—can demonstrate this better way. We can do this together and within our respective traditions.

The world is watching us. What will we show them? Division? Or unity? I am for unity.

WILLIAM D. WATKINS

Theologian, philosopher, apologist, teacher, speaker, and author of numerous publications, including *The New Absolutes*, *The Transformed Habits of a Growing Christian*, *Worlds Apart: A Handbook on World Views*, and, with Keith Fournier, *A House United? Evangelicals and Catholics Together—A Winning Alliance for the 21st Century*

One
SINGLE PIECES OF GLASS

"I do not ask on behalf of these alone, but for those also who believe in Me through their word; that they may all be one; even as You, Father, are in Me and I in You, that they also may be in Us, so that the world may believe that You sent Me."

JOHN 17:20–21

"Glass ... is actually neither a liquid ... nor a solid. It is ... a state somewhere between those two states of matter."[1]

CIARA CURTIN

We had once been an image of the modern nuclear family—mom, dad, and the kids. The children had thrived in their cocoons of innocence. We had seemed solid, like a singular piece of glass. But when the break occurred, our hearts broke too.

In June of 1992, I had just graduated from Penn State as a single mother of five children. It was a triumph to celebrate, but family and financial hardship muted my joy. Yearning to recover from the loss of their father through divorce, first one and then another child had gone to live with him. A physical wound shows; a split heart is harder to see. If we could see it, it would look like cracked glass.

Despair mounted and a practical problem emerged. The amount of child support had been a figure my ex-husband and I had mutually agreed upon; now less support came less often. The children and I had been living on support and student loan money while I finished school. Now, with my degree in hand, I had begun my job search. But at this time, child support was our only income. Even so, money wasn't the cause of my heartache.

Even before my husband left, the children and I were a cohesive unit. We went to church together. We watched movies and went on picnics together. We navigated the grocery store together on a weekly basis. For the first time, we no longer called the same house home.

My broken family was now shattered. For my remaining three children and me, our cupboard became barer and barer. I was now on a first name basis with several bill collectors.

But there was a dim glow on the horizon. Soon a hearing would establish court-ordered support. We just needed to get through a couple of weeks and everything would be okay.

Then a letter arrived explaining that the hearing had been postponed for six more weeks. I took stock of my resources and discovered that someone had given us just the right ingredients to make homemade granola. Unfortunately, I was the only one who wanted to eat it. As the granola became scarce, so did just about everything else, including kitchen staples such as tea and sugar. We had no more peanut butter. The hot dogs were gone too.

So with my kitchen cupboards empty and my support hearing delayed, I sat down at my dining room table and opened my Bible "by chance" to the very short Old Testament book of Habakkuk. There I read of the need to rejoice, even when all resources fail.

Though the fig tree should not blossom
And there be no fruit on the vines,
Though the yield of the olive should fail
And the fields produce no food,
Though the flock should be cut off from the fold
And there be no cattle in the stalls,
Yet I will exult in the LORD,
I will rejoice in the God of my salvation.[2]

Here was a turning point. Would I cry about my lack of goods and let bitterness seal itself in my heart? Or would I rejoice in God and the blessings that remained?

"All right, Lord, I rejoice." Not exactly a resounding shout of praise, but a lesson learned. *Rejoice anyway*—those were the words for that day.

A sense of joy and peace poured over me.

God was reshaping the glass that was me.

Imagine a great stained glass window depicting a man dressed in white with arms outstretched. He faces a woman also dressed in white—a bride.

A Great Master crafted the window, designing the picture and using heat to turn grains of sand into smooth glass to fit perfectly into his bigger picture—each piece just the right color, set in just the right place. Each piece placed to reveal the Master's light and to support the others.

One piece alone is useless. It is fragile, subject to cracking. It conveys no light. But within the window, each piece of glass is part of a glorious picture. Together they tell a love story and present the Master's light. And because of the light pouring through the window, people can become part of the story itself—part of the window shining light to others.

Yet while the image of the man is whole, the image of the woman is imperfect. Someone has thrown stones at her image. Cracks appear in some of her pieces. The Master has fixed some of the damaged panes but cracks still show. And there are shattered places too. Empty places. In some of those empty places the stone thrower has jammed pieces of plastic, distorting the picture. When the weather is cold and stormy, the plastic hardens, breaks, and falls away. But the glass the Master has crafted remains, cracks and all. Still, many people turn away from the spoiled image.

The bride is a picture of the church today.

Satan, the great stone thrower, has fought for the heart and soul of every human since Eden. He has fought for the souls of nations too, including that of America. Christians have worked hard to gain ground in our culture over the last few decades, but today our nation continues to slip further from our biblical roots. In moral peril, our communities and families are the walking wounded. Hurting people without Christ are unrefined grains of sand and often find themselves alone, cracked pieces of solitary glass. As satan aims at hearts, those hearts must be our targets too.

Secular opponents of orthodox Christianity have accused the "Christian Right" of wanting to take America back to the 1950s, to the days of *Ozzie and Harriet, Father Knows Best,* and segregated drinking fountains. We might honestly admit that we dream of past days when teachers led public school students in daily prayer, most children lived with two parents, and terrorism and violence did not appear in daily news reports. We can admit that we would like some aspects of the 1950s without the bigotry and other ills that nostalgia might tempt us to forget.

As much as many of us might like to go back to a society with secure Christian moorings, we now find ourselves in a culture that more closely resembles the world of the first century—with church and state at odds.

Christians were once a small minority in a non-Christian society. And that's what we are becoming today.

Still, we yearn to go back to some fantasy of "the good old days." In those days, we embodied cultural influence. Some, not all of us, experienced greater civility, prosperity, and comfort. But wanting to return to those days moves us in the wrong direction. That road is where Jesus Christ's disciples took their misstep. They initially thought Jesus had come to free them from the rule of the Romans. But the freedom he promised has never been political. The freedom he brings reaches beyond a government's boundaries. Christ calls us to make a difference in the society we have, not the one we wish we had. If the only target of our efforts is the political realm and we neglect the culture around us, society will not change for the better. In fact, decline will continue. Russell Moore, president of the Ethics and Religious Freedom Commission of the Southern Baptist Convention, reminds us that we are "no longer the moral majority. We are a prophetic minority."[3] So we can't move back to the old days, but we can move forward to new days of ministry and service—to days of *less* comfort but greater ministry—and to less discord and more cooperation. Doing so will allow the light of Christ to shine in a way the world has not seen, perhaps, for centuries. It will make the difference he has called us to make.

In the garden before his trial and crucifixion, Christ asked for his followers to "be one." He prayed for those who followed him then and for all who would believe later on—the universal church throughout history.

Many times Jesus prayed to the Father and we have no idea what he said. We're simply told such things as "Jesus Himself would often slip away to the wilderness and pray."[4] Christ and the Father had many moments of communion that the Word does not disclose to us. So every time God's

Word lets us eavesdrop on Christ's side of those conversations, we should pay close attention.

Jesus taught us how to pray with the Lord's Prayer. And through his own prayers, he illustrated his connection and communion with the Father. We hear him blessing the fishes and loaves before crowds and the bread at the Last Supper in the upper room, speaking to the Father before raising Lazarus, before choosing the twelve apostles, and before his transfiguration. We also know he prayed in the garden before his betrayal and arrest. And we hear his prayerful cry from the cross.[5]

Jesus' prayer found in John 17 is the supreme biblical call for accord among his followers. And unlike Paul's letters to singular, local churches, Christ's petition encompasses the worldwide church, for all "those also who believe in Me" through all time.[6] Jesus directs us to love him, each other, and those outside our churches' doors.

Through a series of that/so statements, he tells us what should be (*that*) and what will result from it (*so*).

- *That* we would "all be one" as the Father and Son are "*so* that the world may believe" that the Father sent the Son.

- *That* we "may be perfected" in that oneness "*so* that the world may know" that the Father sent the Son and that He "loved [us], even as the Father loves the Son."

- *That* we would be with Christ where he is *so* that we would see his glory, "which You have given Me, for You loved Me before the foundation of the world."[7]

As Jesus makes clear, the world's ability to know God's love relies upon we who are Christians loving one another in unity.

But it's crucial that we consider what accord is and is not. Christian unity does not mean we dilute our doctrines and abandon our traditions. It does not mean we dissolve our church constitutions and form one gigantic doctrinally devoid church. It means we embrace a visible cooperation with one another—yet without compromise.

> Some suggest [that in his prayer] Jesus is only referring to a nebulous spiritual unity; however, Jesus emphasizes a form of unity that is visible to the watching world, and thus must be referring to a relational unity that can be observed. This does not mean we have to agree on every point of doctrine—we don't! Nor does it mean we are to adopt some sort of fuzzy ecumenism in which we compromise the truth of the gospel or overlook sin within the church.[8]

Journalist and cultural commentator Rod Dreher in his book *The Benedict Option* encourages interdenominational relationships—what he calls "an ecumenism of the trenches." "To be sure, the different churches should not compromise their distinct doctrines, but they should nevertheless seize every opportunity to form friendships and strategic alliances in defense of the faith and the faithful."[9]

Accord means we form friendships and alliances, and we respect each other's differences. It means, as C. S. Lewis wrote, we may "go on disagreeing, but don't let us judge."[10] It means that, at the end of our weekly church services, we join hands to meet real needs and help hurting hearts find healing in Christ—that we *be* the visible church.

But we can only increase our ministry by learning how to meet people in their need.

Likeminded Christians of various denominations acting in accord will enhance ministry. We are the sand the Master turns into colored glass. He restores glass pieces cracked under the pressures of life. And he puts them together in a big picture that shows the world his great love.

We can shine the light of the Master on the hearts of the broken and lonely and invite them to become part of God's big picture.

If you are broken, he can restore you. And once he restores you, he can use you to restore others.

The day after I learned to rejoice no matter what, I retrieved the mail expecting the usual pile of bills I couldn't pay. But buried within the stack was an envelope from Penn State containing a check for $1,300! An accompanying note explained that the money was left over from my student aid account.

In his perfect timing, God's extravagant grace taught me to rejoice— even during dark times—and then filled my need. The children and I made a gleeful visit to the grocery store to restock the kitchen. Everyone got to pick something special, and I paid homage to each bill collector.

A few weeks later, I found part-time employment that eventually grew to full-time. Adding my small paycheck to child support that the court finally ordered, we began to find our feet financially.

There would be more shattering ahead, and we would continue to see meager times. But in this life, there is no end to the lessons God teaches us, the means he uses to teach them to us, and the resources he has at his disposal to meet our needs. Many times our provision came from his people. His church, larger than any building, loved us in our need and helped us escape it.

The moment of our bare cupboard was a low point. The temperature in the furnace I inhabited had peaked—transforming me from sand to glass, from opaque to transparent. Almost liquid and not quite solid, I was his work in his hands. I learned that he shapes his church to display his story.

The church is made up of different pieces of glass—glass of different shades and hues, some with more cracks, some smooth and serene. And some inhabit pews unlike my own. But they are people also living to follow Christ, also urging others to follow him too.

If you're shattered like a piece of glass
The more broke you are the more the light gets through.[11]

JASON GRAY

{Endnotes}

1   Ciara Curtin, "Fact or Fiction?: Glass Is a (Supercooled) Liquid: Are Medieval Windows Melting?" *Scientific American*, February 22, 2007, https://www.scientificamerican.com/article/fact-fiction-glass-liquid.

2   Habakkuk 3:17–18.

3   Naomi Schaefer Riley, "Russell Moore: From Moral Majority to Prophetic Minority," *Wall Street Journal, August 16, 2013, https://www.wsj.com/articles/russell-moore-from-moral-majority-to-prophetic-minority-1376694815.*

4   Luke 5:16.

5   Jesus teaching the Lord's Prayer (Matthew 6:9–13), his prayer intimacy with the Father (11:25–26), his blessing of food (14:19; 15:37; 26:26), his prayer around raising Lazarus (John 11:41–42), and his prayers before choosing the apostles (Luke 6:12–13), before his transfiguration (9:29), during his time in the garden (Matthew 26:36–44; Luke 22:39–46), and from his position on the cross (Matthew 27:46; Mark 15:37; Luke 23:34, 46).

6   John 17:20.

7   John 17:21–23.

8   S. Michael Craven, "Practical Unity: Living Out the Words of Jesus to 'Be One,'" *Christianity Today, May 14, 2014.*

9   Rod Dreher, *The Benedict Option: A Strategy for Christians in a Post-Christian Nation (New York: Sentinel, 2017), 136.*

10   C. S. Lewis, *Letters of C. S. Lewis, as quoted in an email from the C. S. Lewis Foundation, January 23, 2015.*

11   Jason Gray, vocalist, "Glow in the Dark," Jason Gray and Ben Glover, *Where the Light Gets In, Centricity Songs and Graybird Songs (BMI) / Universal Music-Brentwood Benson Pub, and D Soul Music (ASCAP), 2015, http://www.klove.com/music/artists/jason-gray/songs/glow-in-the-dark-lyrics.aspx.*

Two
BROKEN FAMILY,
CRACKED GLASS

"'For the Lord has called you,
Like a wife forsaken and grieved in spirit,
Even like a wife of one's youth when she is rejected,' says your God."

ISAIAH 54:6

"It is paradoxical that textural imperfections in glass ...
tend to make the glass more attractive." [1]

THE STAINED GLASS ASSOCIATION OF AMERICA

Motherhood is an imperfect, constantly changing state. It's a gradual shift from birthing a newborn to perhaps having more. Newborns become toddlers who become teens. And finally, if things go well, they become adults, and the connections a family forges over the years remain strong.

The best job I ever had was being mommy. I baked cookies, kissed booboos, and designed trick-or-treat costumes. I made hot chocolate for sledding children who would bound through the door with flushed cheeks and tales of mountain conquests. Oh, it wasn't all fun. There were harried treks to church, sibling conflicts, ear infections, sibling conflicts, stomach flus, and sibling conflicts. But there were also picnics with modified baseball gear, a whiffle ball bat, and a tennis ball. We made a mosaic of memories.

And then we broke.

The term *broken family* means a parent is missing because of divorce. Someone's choice fractured society's smallest community. A family who has had a parent die is not a broken family, even though an important person is missing. That kind of family is sad too, but the children don't shuttle between parents on the weekends. They don't live with two sets of rules and values. And they don't watch the warfare in which they themselves become unwilling weapons.

Until it happened to me, I never dreamed I would be a single mother. But here I was. Rather, here we were—five children and me. We had gone from a place we thought was stable and secure to a new reality— uncertainty. We cracked, broke, then shattered.

Our road was dark, but Christian companions walked with us, and Christian communities lit our path. These companions were not from a singular church body but from various congregations from different traditions. Each friend pursued the same goal—to follow Christ and to encourage us to do the same. In so doing, they prepared our hearts to minister to others later.

Our story represents the stories of many other American families today, broken by divorce. But what we became for a time represents a microcosm of today's church, separated through disagreement and misunderstanding.

Many evangelicals perceive that liturgical traditions—Roman Catholicism, Orthodoxy, and some Protestant denominations—are steeped in empty ritual. Many liturgical believers perceive that evangelicalism is steeped in empty emotion. Liturgical and evangelical traditions both claim allegiance to the roots of the early church. Both contain true believers, not merely those who are church members or intellectual assenters, but those who respond to Christ's call to follow him with total commitment.

True believers from every denomination see ourselves as divided when we are really merely separated. There is a crucial difference between separation and division. Since we who have committed to following Christ believe in the same God and in his power and ability to redeem us, we are not divided. Separation often happens as we become judgmental about the ways our worship differs in our following the same God. Division, however, happens when someone chooses to follow a path that denies who God is and that we are accountable to him for how we live our lives. When such deviation takes place, division becomes necessary because separation has already occurred.

I had not chosen divorce. I had, however, insisted on separation. A broken covenant sometimes requires separation. An unhealthy environment requires change. For the next three years, I waited for my husband to resolve the situation by choosing either reconciliation or permanent division. Ultimately, the separation between us became division when he chose divorce and remarriage.

Because of our broken covenant and his new covenant, the division between my ex-husband and me is permanent and appropriate. Division must remain division. Civility can accompany it, but there can be no reunion. On the other hand, for the children and me, where separation existed, it would be impermanent. Separation can turn into healing, accord, and deep love.

In the same way, an appropriate division exists between Christians who name Jesus as Lord and those who carry the name *Christian* but think of Jesus as only a great teacher, not *the* Great Teacher, Savior, and Lord.

Separation, on the other hand, exists among those who name Jesus as Lord but cannot see past differences to affirm his name in cooperative ministry. Real glass abides with real glass, even if there is separation. Real glass and fake glass don't inhabit the same window—at least not for long. Fake glass has no lasting power. Eventually, a breaking point arrives.

In the same way, it's never just one event that leads a couple to divorce. Many elements develop into divorce—authentic disagreement, misunderstandings, self-centeredness—sins that easily entangle us[2]—obstacles only a truly unified couple can overcome.

Our unwillingness to see beyond our own viewpoints is the biggest culprit. It leads us to entangling sins. Those sins lead to brokenness. Brokenness in a family limits its ability to minister even to its own members, let alone to those outside itself. Broken people are wounded people who need healing. Broken people are cracked glass.

Jesus Christ's instrument to bring that healing is his church, but today's church is its own broken family. We accuse each other of being fake glass without checking for authenticity.

The great evangelists from Wesley to Moody and from Billy Sunday to Billy Graham poured themselves out to deliver the message that God is personal, seeking relationship with us. For Orthodox Christians, "the personal relationship with God is *everything*. ... [I]t is about entering into a radically subjective relationship with the living God—something that has been central to Christianity since the beginning."[3] And Catholic apologist George Weigel asserts that true Catholicism is a relationship in which a believer "*knows* Jesus."[4]

Apologists from all three Christian traditions—Orthodox, Catholic, and Protestant—assert that their form of Christianity embodies the fullest form of truth about God. But the better part of all three branches grant that each of the other Christian traditions has some understanding of God's truth. All three traditions also acknowledge that those in relationship with Christ will sin, but they must resist sin and pursue obedience. These three traditions understand that no one can be in relationship with Christ and willfully and continuously live in sin and disobedience. In short, all three traditions assert that God is a personal God, that believers must be in relationship with him, and that relationship with God requires obedience. Relationship and obedience: most of us haven't realized that we agree on these key factors (as well as on many others). Realizing we have significant areas of agreement can lead us to accord.

Besides Christ's prayer in the upper room, several biblical passages encourage us to pursue accord. Speaking to singular, local church bodies, the apostle Paul exhorted the Corinthians, the Ephesians, and the Colossians to avoid separation in their midst.[5] Paul called believers in various locations to remain faithful morally and doctrinally, which would help maintain their unity in Christ.

On the other hand, division in the church may be needed at times. And in the first century, it became necessary. For example, division was necessary for the Corinthians dealing with sin. Paul pointed out there was "immorality among you, and immorality of such a kind as does not exist even among the Gentiles, that someone has his father's wife." Such grievous sin would mandate that the offenders "be removed from your midst" unless they repented.[6]

Today separation happens over differing doctrines, different ways of viewing baptism, communion, and the saints—even as we agree about sin. Separation without moral imperative has weakened ministry. It has kept us from seeing the beauty of each other's traditions and how seeing that beauty can effect accord and bring about ministry. Let's consider a few pages from literature. Perhaps they can show us the beauty we can infuse into our daily Christian walk and our pursuit of accord.

Evangelical Christians emphasize *individual* faith. In *The Pilgrim's Progress*, John Bunyan's character Christian walks a lone journey of faith.[7] From time to time, he has companions, good and bad. The good walk beside him and encourage him, and the bad try to divert him from his way. His ultimate goal is to arrive at the Celestial City, or Zion, which represents eternal life in heaven.

While Christian has various companions, his walk is primarily solitary. He has no sustained community with him throughout his journey. The encouragement Christian's godly companions give him illustrates his need for community. Christian makes the final leg of his journey with the companionship of another character, Hopeful. The two share the experience of death represented in crossing the river. Each encourages the other as they maneuver the river individually. Bunyan—as does the Protestant perspective—focuses on the individual journey of faith. Communion is not the focus of Christian's walk.

Conversely, Catholicism and Eastern Orthodoxy emphasize the communion of members. The Catholic journey is not solitary. J. R. R. Tolkien's *The Lord of the Rings* books show us the journey of Frodo Baggins.[8] He must destroy the ring that empowers evil, and only he can do that. Even though this mission falls to him, he is still part of a community. Members in his group assist him on his way, sometimes working in separate locations. Yet their quest is united; their efforts aim toward one goal—helping Frodo destroy the evil ring. Unlike Christian's journey, Frodo's expedition is anything but solitary. The evil of the ring draws in and tempts various characters, but working together, they see good triumph. When one becomes weak, another is strong to help him through difficulty. The community of good must overcome the army of evil and that is exactly what they accomplish.

Both Bunyan's Christian and Tolkien's Frodo face horrific challenges, suffer terrible defeats, and experience exhilarating victories. Both represent Christ's followers. Each story presents a different Christian perspective, but neither story violates orthodoxy. To be evangelical, like Christian, is to follow God as you associate with companion believers who help you on your way. To be Catholic or Orthodox, like Frodo, is to walk as part of a believing community as you follow God.

Companions and community—that is who we, the church, are.

To be clear, Catholicism and Orthodoxy also encourage individual faith and ministry, and Protestant evangelicalism encourages community ministry. In all three traditions, *individuals* come to belief. In all three traditions, *community* is important. The difference is a matter of emphasis.

Twenty-five years after Tolkien, William E. Barrett published *The Lilies of the Field*.[9] This novella weaves Bunyan's and Tolkien's perspectives in a beautiful tale of Homer Smith, a lone, African-American, Baptist, traveling handyman. Homer builds a chapel at the behest of a Catholic community of nuns headed by a stern, German mother superior—Mother Maria Marthe. She refers to Homer as Schmidt. Homer calls her Old Mother. He drives the nuns to Mass every Sunday morning and teaches them English. With money he earns at a second job, he buys them groceries until their garden begins to produce a harvest. Homer and Old Mother butt heads more than once. They work hard to overcome their language differences and the constant siren call of the road that rings in Homer's ears. The nuns are planted in community; Homer yearns to get on his singular way.

After completing the chapel, Homer resumes his journey on his way to a "settling-down time"—his Zion.[10] The Catholic community he leaves behind prospers and grows, inspired by the man Mother describes as "not of our faith, nor of our skin ... but a man of greatness, of an utter devotion."[11]

The nuns in Mother's community willingly share their meager supplies with Homer. He shares his meager earnings with the community of nuns. Community and companion give of themselves. Barrett merges two faith perspectives in a story that shapes Homer Smith's spirit and Mother Maria Marthe's community.

Becoming available to walk with someone else in service to Christ at any given time provides opportunities for the ministry of companionship. Companionship can be messy and inconvenient. Even though our modern lives are hectic, we can be companions to those God places in our path, those in need of prayer, encouragement, and example. Our effort may involve a momentary inconvenience or immense personal sacrifice.

Community ministry also requires prayer and personal sacrifice, but in communal ministry, we are part of a team. Communities can be small and loosely structured, or large and well structured. They are not necessarily denominational authorities; they are usually individual believers coming together.

Individual ministry allows us to help those within the image of the window and those outside it. Community ministry allows us to join hands with anyone within the picture, regardless of faith tradition. Both kinds of ministry make the image of the window clearer. And so we present Christ and the Bride to a world that deeply misunderstands the Christian faith.

We become one "so that the world may know." Thus, we can bring hope and wholeness to the shattered. We can help them find their place in the window.

From a practical standpoint, accord also means we can better learn where needs exist and where some services are wanting and others duplicated. We become a nurturing presence within ministry communities. We work to meet needs in effective ways, freeing people from dependence on charity and government programs that can trap them in a net of dependence. That's just part of what I learned through our time of need. My children learned it too. God used people of faith to help us cross the gulf between dependence on government assistance to reliance on God.

The year 2017 marked five hundred years since Martin Luther's protest in 1517. We stand at a crossroad in history. The winds of hostility toward our faith are sighing and gaining speed. We can continue to hang on to our differences, or we can embrace a heart of cooperation within our diversity of traditions. If we do the latter, we can show charity, another word for love, as we go forward, and it's this love that fixes cracked glass. Fixing involves a different kind of breaking—it's shaping that fits us for our place in the picture. And as parts of the picture, we rely on the Master—and each other.

RIPPLES

A stone dropped in water makes ripples that unfold across years,
Forever changing the world.
Words we consider insignificant make ripples others
drink for generations,
Enduring lessons the child carries to those coming later,
Lessons that cause wounds or bring healing.
A cup of cold water for a child in His name
Stops thirst, fills souls.

{Endnotes}

1   The Stained Glass Association of America, "Glass for Stained Glass," SGAA online, 2012, http://stainedglass.org.

2   Hebrews 12:1.

3   Rod Dreher, "Catholics and the 'Personal Relationship' with God," *The American Conservative*, May 12, 2014, http://www.theamericanconservative.com/dreher/catholics-the-personal-relationship-with-god/comment-page-1.

4   George Weigel, *Evangelical Catholicism: Deep Reform in the 21st-Century Church* (New York: Basic Books, 2013), 57, Weigel's emphasis.

5   1 Corinthians 1:10; 11:17–19; 12:12–25; Ephesians 4:1–3, 13; Colossians 3:14.

6   1 Corinthians 5:1–2.

7   John Bunyan, *The Pilgrim's Progress: From This World to That Which Is to Come; Delivered under the Similitude of a Dream*, Gutenberg.org, first published, 1678.

8   J. R. R. Tolkien, *The Lord of the Rings* series: *The Fellowship of the Ring*, *The Two Towers*, and *The Return of the King*.

9   William E, Barrett, *Lilies of the Field* (New York: Warner, 1995; first published, 1962).

10   Ibid., 119.

11   Ibid., 127.

Three
SHATTERED FAMILY, SHAPED GLASS

"The sacrifices of God are a broken spirit; A broken and a contrite heart, O God, You will not despise."

PSALM 51:17

"Glass cutting is actually a controlled fracture process. The cutting wheel rolls along the glass surface, scoring it and producing stress patterns within the glass which help to guide the break to be made."[1]

CLAUDE LIPS

There are two ways to break glass. One is to simply shatter it. The other is to score it, guide the break, and shape the glass for beauty and function. God's hands reshape shattered hearts and rebuild broken lives for placement in the picture of his story.

Being broken can hurt. But God can use our brokenness to glorify himself.

Being broken can be bad, but it can be good too. We rejoice in the good and move beyond the bad.

My husband left in February of 1985. On a Friday evening, we told the children he was leaving so they would have the weekend to rally a bit before they had to go back to school. On Monday morning, we put on the suit of our old family routine, but it no longer fit. Our parents and my brother knew what was happening, but beyond our closest circle, we didn't tell anyone else right away.

The children and I were hurt and embarrassed and dreamed of a grand reunion that would take us back to life as it had been—back to normal. We wanted to patch the glass, and we hoped no one would notice the bumpy places, the pasted over cracks. But reunion didn't happen, and little by little the news got out. I dreaded running into acquaintances at a store or at church. I put up a sturdy façade: I was fine—great, in fact. But I remember a look in the eye, a look of pity and pain. People felt I had been wronged; I felt wronged too. I also felt like a failure. I had failed at marriage.

A great expanse planted itself between my new life and my old one. I was willing to go back, but that landscape no longer existed. Forward or backward, either would be a new place. From now on, our family would have two histories. We would have two sets of stories that would sometimes touch but not quite intertwine.

A great expanse of separation also exists between our various faith communities, but it is a space we can traverse. Accord is possible because, although we don't seem to realize it, we already rely on the wisdom of each other's traditions.

Many evangelical Protestant leaders love to quote Augustine, Blaise Pascal, G. K. Chesterton, and Malcolm Muggeridge, all Catholics, as well as Alexander Solzhenitsyn, an Orthodox believer, and liturgical Protestants Dietrich Bonhoeffer and C. S. Lewis. We evangelicals love their devotion to God, their wisdom, their clarity of voice in speaking truth. And yet, because of various beliefs each of them held, none of them would qualify for membership in a typical evangelical church today. We receive these fathers of the faith from a distance, loving the light they shine as they still speak to us and ignoring the lesser points on which we disagree. We have a sense of fellowship with these men. Rather, we imagine a fellowship with the idea of them, the idea that they were just like us. Actually, they were unlike us in many ways, but the similarities we share with them draw us to their counsel. Still, many evangelicals separate themselves from the faith descendants of these great men. Consequently, we remain distant from those who hold convictions similar to ours.

In spite of the church schisms that occurred before Luther (there were four),[2] Chesterton asserts that "Christianity was shattered at the Reformation."[3] No schism can destroy the church itself, for even "the gates of Hades shall not overcome" the church.[4] Chesterton's point, however, is viable when we consider that each schism increased the number of subgroups within Christianity. And the Protestant Reformation produced the greatest number of subgroups.

Where one group defies essential doctrine, division is necessary. But where essential doctrines are affirmed, accord can end separation.

The distinctions are easy to understand when we look at Calvinism and Methodism. Calvin emphasized election—the predestined state of believers. Methodism's founder, John Wesley, emphasized the choice or free will of the believer. Neither election nor free will is a small matter to a Calvinist or a Methodist. Yet both forms of Christianity believe salvation comes from Christ alone. Accord asks us not to overlook such perspectives but to join hands even as we engage in robust but respectful discussion about our areas of disagreement.

As different denominations adopted, not only different areas of emphasis, but also various styles of worship, splits turned into shattering.

The separation between Catholicism and Protestantism has resulted in a vast number of sects with various practices.

Establishing new sects sparked both negative and positive results. One negative has been that churches "have ostracized each other for centuries, leaving a legacy of deep divisions and resentments." That statement comes from *Christianity: Fundamental Teachings*. The book was a collaborative effort of Orthodox, Catholic, and Protestant leaders in Turkey—an overwhelmingly Muslim country with a tiny minority of Christians. When Turkey's Christians realized that government textbooks failed to accurately explain basic Christianity, their effort began to fill this need. It took ten years for the various participants to agree on a ninety page book explaining the basic tenets of Christianity.[5] The challenge to accurately represent the faith in a hostile environment overcame centuries of disagreement over issues all sides consider important. They simply decided that representing Christ to those who might never otherwise understand his truth was more important than their differences.

Much of the world interprets our disagreement over doctrine as a lack of love for each other. This interpretation is the glue on the back of the label the world pastes on our faith. The front of the label clearly states, "Hypocrites"—people who talk about love but refuse to love each other.

It might be surprising to learn that the shattering in and after the Reformation also produced positive results. While no corner of Christianity has been able to avoid some blot of corruption, just as no one human is free of sin, the Catholic church today is free of one of Luther's main complaints—the selling of indulgences.[6]

But the idea that the church allowed and encouraged the sale of indulgences is a distortion of Catholicism that lingers today. Nowhere in the Bible, nor in Catholic teaching, does God promise to grant special favors for financial donations. Indulgences are not forgiveness, and

Catholic teaching does not (and never did) claim that indulgences affect anyone's eternal destiny.[7]

Selling indulgences parallels a practice common in many evangelical organizations today—that of promising God's favor for contributions, otherwise known as the prosperity gospel. Christians may indeed receive blessings for their obedience in giving, but the only appropriate motives for giving are obedience and a desire to bring blessings to others. Anytime we give in order to get, our motives are impure; our gift is defiled.

While there is disagreement among the traditions as to how God's grace manifests itself, Catholicism, Orthodoxy, and evangelicalism all reject the notion that anyone can "buy" salvation with works. On the day of accounting, Jesus will not say that the lost did not work hard enough or that they did not exercise enough faith. He will say, "I never *knew* you; depart from Me you who practice lawlessness."[8]

A works-based rather than grace-based salvation would prompt selfish motives for doing good. Instead, liturgical traditions assert that good works result from God's leading and grace. Evangelicals agree that the good we do does not come from within our hearts without God's influence. True Christ followers understand that to base our lives on the pattern of Christ's life is not a ticket to easy street. It's a call to sacrifice.

Yet the Catholic/Orthodox view of salvation can differ from the evangelical view. The evangelical view often encompasses a one-time commitment: once saved, always saved. (Disputes over the nature of salvation have contributed to increased splintering within evangelicalism.) The liturgical view tends to see salvation as a process that unfolds throughout life and includes the believer's cooperation with God's grace.

> The teaching of the New Testament is that God's grace, our free will, and our faith and good works, are intimately connected. The Holy Spirit energizes in us

both faith and good works as we thirst for and seek God's grace. Neither faith nor good works can be presented as merit before God, but only as return gifts in humility, love, and thanksgiving. Let us not forget as well the sober words of James: "Faith by itself, if it has no works, is dead ... Faith is completed by works ... A person is justified by works and not by faith alone" (James 2:17, 22, 24). By free will, faith, and earnest labors, we work together with the grace of God in the awesome gift and mystery of salvation.[9]

Neither Catholicism nor Orthodoxy embraces a works-based salvation independent of God's grace. And all three traditions hold that a profession of faith that does not produce the fruit of works is not a true conversion.

Ending the sale of indulgences was not the only positive outcome of the shattering of the church into various denominations. Increasing the number of Christian traditions also increased the number of Christ followers available to carry the message of light into a dark world. A related example occurs in the book of Acts when Paul and Barnabas disagreed. Paul wanted to visit towns where they had already preached and check on the churches. Barnabas agreed but wanted to take John Mark along. Paul didn't trust John Mark who had previously abandoned them. "So sharp was their disagreement that they separated."[10] Instead of one evangelistic team, they became two.

The more workers who spread the message, the more opportunities to proclaim the gospel to those who've not heard of Christ—and the more opportunities to disciple new followers. Perhaps God allowed our separation in order to shine the light of the good news about his Son more broadly in the world.

But this illumination process has a cycle to it. It's the principle of diminishing returns. When the gospel is new to an unchurched area, Christianity flourishes. But once the good news is established where comfort is plentiful, competition and discord between traditions set in. Churches cease to produce new Christians. Instead of a quest to enlighten the unchurched, different denominations end up trading members instead of making new ones. When proclaiming the gospel becomes competition for members, separation becomes bitter and accord unlikely.

The history of Christianity in Korea illustrates how accord thrives under duress and how separation comes with familiarity and wealth. Christianity was born in Korea without missionaries or clergy. God sparked this remarkable feat through the efforts of Catholic missionaries who went to China in the sixteenth century. Nearly two centuries later, Korean ambassadors visiting Peking (now Beijing) found books Jesuit missionaries had distributed. The books were useful to the Koreans because, while the Chinese and Korean spoken languages were different, the written languages were the same. One of these ambassadors converted and returned to Korea where he led many to the Christian faith. Years later, the first Catholic missionary to Korea was Chinese. Upon his arrival, he discovered four thousand already baptized believers waiting for him.[11]

Persecution afflicted the Korean church since its inception.[12] Over time, the torment worsened. Korea had taken an isolationist stance and was hostile to foreigners—missionaries and traders alike.[13] In the nineteenth century, Robert Jermain Thomas became the first Protestant missionary to minister in this hostile land. Thomas came to Korea from China where he had met two Catholic Koreans desperate to have copies of the Bible.[14] So he went to Korea with a supply of God's Word. A Korean Catholic helped Thomas learn the local dialect to support him in his efforts to "announce to these poor people some of the most precious truths of the Gospel."[15]

In Korea, two traditions worked in unity. At that time, "the distinctions between the Catholic Church and the Protestant Church were less evident in China and Korea than [they were] in Europe."[16] Ministry in accord showed pagan Koreans the story of the Bride Church and the Groom Savior through the light of the stained glass window. Thomas and the Korean Catholics were different colored glass pieces depicting that picture through ministry.

And that ministry required Christ-like sacrifice.

Thomas handed a Bible to the soldier waiting to execute him and became the first Protestant martyr in Korea. Many Catholic martyrs had gone before him. Thomas and the Catholic believers he met could have eyed each other with suspicion and refused to help each other. But under the horrors of persecution, they joined forces, and Christianity grew in Korea.

About thirty years after Thomas' mission to Asia began, Russian Orthodox clergy established a missional effort in Korea.[17] Now all three traditions were present on the peninsula. During the first half of the twentieth century, Japan occupied Korea. Christian leaders supported efforts to gain independence from Japan, sparking "rapid growth" in the church, which the Japanese tried to quash.[18]

Because different denominations sent multiple missionaries to Korea (a positive, unintended result of the Reformation), more workers were available to explain the true God. Even with varying methods of worship, Christianity spread across Korea. Sending many workers from various denominations was effective as long as the pool of potential converts was non-Christian.

However, after World War II, a civil war split Korea into two parts. In the southern half, Christianity flourished and free enterprise blossomed. Along with freedom came prosperity and comfort. Today, South Korean denominations compete against each other for members. The South Korean church has few new converts to Christianity.

> Given the long history of competition between the Catholic and Protestant communities in [South] Korea and scant goodwill between them, it is unlikely that their sibling rivalry will end anytime soon ... . Meanwhile, on the sidelines, Buddhists will enjoy watching the continuing competition between those two Christian groups while their community grows as well, ensuring that a substantial proportion of the religion-oriented population of the Republic of Korea remains non-Christian.[19]

At the same time in the north, however, the faithful live in the "worst country [in which] to be a Christian."[20] They understand aspects of the Christian faith that we in more comfortable countries often miss. About one third of the one hundred thousand North Korean Christians reside in concentration camps. Within those camps, they remain "steadfast in their faith, even sharing it with others."[21] These believers simply share the gospel rather than competing against a different presentation of it.

Competition increases separation. It shatters in a way that's difficult to overcome. On the other hand, persecution drives church growth and accord. It doesn't shatter Christian unity. It shapes cut glass to make it useful and beautiful. Persecution seeks to break the window, but it only serves to strengthen the glass, to clarify the picture.

The image of a cracked church is unclear. Sometimes it results from legitimate disagreement. Sometimes from misunderstanding and pride.

The Circle of Us

We start by understanding that there is Truth.
We see our sin and realize God is our only hope.
We encounter him and find joy.
We find a small circle of others like us and settle
   into comfort.
We feel good about us.

We forget our sin and unworthiness;
We forget God wants us to wash feet,
Carry a cross,
Follow in his steps.
We feel good about us.

We see others' sins, but not their wounds, their needs.
We look hard at their sins;
We forget our own.
Our little circle is snug.
We feel good about us.

{ENDNOTES}

1   Claude Lips, *Art and Stained Glass* (New York: Doubleday, 1973), 33.

2   Around 385, the first schism occurred when Arians separated from the orthodox church, affirming that Jesus was an eternally created being who created everything else in the world and was subordinate to the eternal, uncreated God the Father. The next schism happened near 435 when Nestorians went their own way, claiming that while Jesus was fully human and fully divine, the union between his two natures was one of will only; his natures were not united in one Person, the Son of God. Around 533, Monophysites left the orthodox church, contending that Jesus' humanity and deity meshed to create a third, single nature that was neither human nor divine. The fourth schism was far more significant than the previous three, for it tore the church of the East from the church of the West in 1054. The causes of this split are far too many to mention here, but they led to the patriarch of Constantinople and the pope of Rome excommunicating each other. See Henry Chadwick, *The Early Church*, rev. ed. (London: The Penguin Group, 1993), chs. 8–9 and 14; Alan Schreck, *The Compact History of the Catholic Church* (Ann Arbor: Servant Books, 1987), ch. 2; Timothy Ware, *The Orthodox Church*, rev. ed. (New York: Penguin Group, 1997), chs. 2–3; William G. T. Shedd, *A History of Christian Doctrine*, 9th ed. (Minneapolis: Klock & Klock, 1979, reprint ed.; original ed., 1889), vol. 1, ch. 5; J. N. D. Kelly, *Early Christian Doctrines*, rev. ed. (San Francisco: Harper & Row, 1978), chs. 9–12; and Louis Berkhof, *The History of Christian Doctrines* (Grand Rapids: Baker Book House, 1937), 83–112.

3   G. K. Chesterton, *Orthodoxy* (Chicago: Moody, 2009; first published, 1908), 50.

4   Matthew 16:18.

5   Barbara G. Baker, "Turkey's Churches, Famous for Historic Schism, Finally Agree on Doctrine," *Christianity Today*, April 2, 2018, https://www.christianitytoday.com/news/2018/april/turkey-churches-agree-on-doctrine-christian-book.html.

6   Indulgences involve the remission of temporary consequences of sins. Those consequences could occur in one's life or after death and coincide with the doctrine of purgatory.

7   Catholic Answers, "Myths about Indulgences," August 10, 2004, https://www.catholic.com/tract/myths-about-indulgences.

8   Matthew 7:23, emphasis added.

9   Fr. Theodore Stylianopoulos, "How Are We Saved?," Greek Orthodox Archdiocese of America, November 2, 2012, https://www.goarch.org/-/how-are-we-saved-.

10   Acts 15:36.

11   Brian Kelly, "The Church in Korea, Founded by Sages, Not Missionaries," Catholicism.org, July 15, 2014, http://catholicism.org/the-church-in-korea-founded-by-sages-not-missionaries.html.

12   Ibid.

13   Stella Price, *Chosen for Choson (Korea)*, 2nd ed. (Exeter: Emmaus Road Ministries, 2010), 54–55.

14   Ibid., 46.

15   Ibid., 50.

16   Ibid., 54.

17   Ware, *The Orthodox Church*, 189.

18   Byong-suh Kim, "Modernization and the Explosive Growth and Decline of Korean Protestant Religiosity," as quoted in Robert E. Buswell Jr. and Timothy S. Lee, eds., *Christianity in Korea* (Honolulu: University of Hawaii Press, 2006), 317.

19   Donald Baker, "Sibling Rivalry in Twentieth-Century Korea: Comparative Growth Rates of Catholics and Protestants," as quoted in Buswell Jr. and Lee, *Christianity in Korea*, 304–305.

20   Olivia Enos, "North Korea Is the World's Worst Persecutor of Christians," *Forbes*, January 25, 2017, https://www.forbes.com/sites/oliviaenos/2017/01/25/north-korea-is-the-worlds-worst-persecutor-of-christians/#153c9eb8318e.

21   Carey Lodge, "North Korea: Where Christians Are Persecuted but Strong in Faith," *Christianity Today*, June 25, 2014, https://www.christiantoday.com/article/north-korea-where-christians-are-persecuted-but-strong-in-faith/38410.htm.

Four
DIFFERENT COLORED GLASS

"But the wisdom from above is first pure, then peaceable, gentle, reasonable, full of mercy and good fruits, unwavering, without hypocrisy. And the seed whose fruit is righteousness is sown in peace by those who make peace."

JAMES 3:17–18

"There is a common thread in the whole history of color in art, as I saw in those cathedral windows ... the vital role played by imperfection, accident, and vulnerability in the striving for perfection."[1]

VICTORIA FINLAY

Imperfect glass loving other imperfect glass. Navigating the same road of vulnerability. Stumbling into providential accident. Walking a path out of darkness toward the light that pours through the window of us. That is our lifelong journey in the church.

Stained glass windows show us different colors that complement each other.

My father, George, was the sixth of eleven children growing up in East Liverpool, Ohio. Orphaned by the time he was thirteen years old, he was the only one of his siblings to finish high school and go to college. A pharmacy student in the middle of his college years when the Japanese attacked Pearl Harbor, Dad enlisted in the navy. He was a natural for the medical corps, served with US Marine Seabee construction units in the South Pacific, and achieved the rank of chief petty officer.

My mother, Nan, the daughter of a bricklayer, also grew up in East Liverpool. Mom's only brother died after World War II ended while his army unit was still in Europe. He had survived the war only to have his jeep run off the road by an American truck driver. Mom had not waited out the war at home. Trained as a medical secretary, she joined the US Coast Guard and served in Oklahoma—strangely so, it seems, since Oklahoma has no coast to guard.

Dad was a Catholic; Mom was a Methodist. Both my parents were heartfelt in their faith in God, if sporadic in their church participation. By the end of their lives, their devotion to God had grown. Mom answered an altar call before her death at age fifty-four. When Dad was older, he prayed on his knees every day before dementia overtook him. He referred to these sessions as conversations with Jesus.

Neither of my parents had an easy time growing up. Many of their years as parents were difficult as well. Finances were tight during the inflationary seventies. Mom's illness meant her contributions to the family were limited. These troubles made their marriage all the more admirable. They didn't stay together *because* it was so easy. They stayed together because they were committed, even though it *wasn't* easy. Their lives carried the hues from different backgrounds. They each carried their own cracks.

But they shared a view of life and faith that kept them committed to one another and to us children. From different religious backgrounds, they still shared a singular perspective.

A singular perspective of faith marked the early days of the Christian church. Accord prevailed until separation came. Protestants and Catholics have been arguing for five hundred years since Luther, but differences between Catholic and Orthodox believers go back a thousand years to 1054 when the Great Schism between the Western church and the Eastern church occurred. The divide happened mainly over two points of dispute.

The first was the authority of the pope. Catholics claimed that the bishop of Rome, the pope, had authority over all of Christendom. Orthodox Christians in the East claimed he did not. That point of separation is easy to see.

The second dispute centers around the *filioque*, a Latin term meaning "and the Son." It's a phrase Orthodoxy claims the Roman Church added to the Nicene Creed and that Catholicism claims Orthodoxy removed. The argument is not over the reality of the Trinity; it's a dispute about the "eternal relations within the Godhead."[2] It's not a small question to either side, and both sides claim the support of Scripture in the discussion.

These differences—the authority of the pope and the relationships within the divine persons of the Trinity—are authentic points of disagreement.

Yet the Great Schism was not the first point of separation for Christianity.

Having begun in the Middle East and spread west into Europe, the church endured a split about fifteen hundred years ago—the Monophysite schism. On one side were Oriental Orthodox, comprised of churches in the Middle East, including those in Armenia, India, and Egypt. (Orthodox Christians in Egypt are Coptic Christians.) This group of churches separated from what is now Eastern (Greek or Russian) Orthodoxy.[3] This dispute wasn't over an authentic point of disagreement but was simply a misunderstanding.

The two sides met speaking different languages—Greek and Latin. Their discussion centered on the nature of Christ. The Latin (Roman) side came to a wrong conclusion about the beliefs on the Greek side.

> The Roman and Constantinopolitan (Latin) delegates incorrectly believed the Coptic and other Oriental Orthodox churches said Christ had only one nature [essentially one nature at a time]. The church as a whole insisted that Jesus had two natures — human and divine — that existed at the same time. What the Coptic churches and their compatriots actually said was Christ's two natures were inseparable. In other words, Jesus was always fully human and always fully God. The Oriental Orthodox mistakenly believed the rest of the [Greek] delegates insisted Jesus had two distinct natures that were separated from one another. In other words, Jesus was sometimes God and sometimes not God.[4]

So all believed that Jesus was wholly God and wholly man all the time during his Incarnation and afterward, but the split happened because of a bad translation. They were saying the same thing but misunderstood each other's languages.

It took a long time before both sides acknowledged that they agreed about the nature of Christ. In 1973 (Catholic) Pope Paul VI and (Coptic Orthodox) Alexandrian Pope Shenouda III met and issued a joint statement: "Jesus Christ is perfect God with respect to His divinity, perfect man with respect to His humanity. In Him, His divinity is united with His humanity in a real, perfect union."⁵ The meeting opened the door to discussion between the two groups, and the door remains open today.⁶

A dialogue has begun between liturgical traditions, but separation still defines the church more than accord does. The reasons for our separation are many. Some involve authentic areas of disagreement, such as those between Catholicism and Orthodoxy over the authority of the pope and the interworking of the Trinity. Others involve misunderstanding of beliefs, like the split within Orthodoxy. Misunderstanding prevents the kind of ministry that Robert Thomas and his Catholic counterparts shared in Korea. Misunderstanding can harden our hearts and lead us to wrong judgments.

News and social media alike were ablaze over the twenty-one Egyptian Christians (Coptics) whom ISIS terrorists beheaded early in 2015. The persecution of these Christians, whose misunderstood doctrine sparked the third separation of the church, is long and storied. Fond of showing videos of their atrocities, ISIS did not edit out the singing of the victims who proclaimed their love for Christ to the end.

In response to the outcry of admiration for these Christian martyrs, one critic repeated the original mistranslation, listed other misunderstandings, and then concluded that the Egyptian martyrs were "not Christians":

> Is it being born into an ethnic group that denies the dual-nature of Christ in his full deity and humanity? Is it embracing a meritorious, works-based salvation nearly identical to that of the Roman Catholic church [*sic*]? Is it in aggressively denying salvation by a personal, saving relationship with Jesus Christ? We ask because that's

> what Coptic 'Christians' believe. This really isn't new,
> and we have to wonder why our leaders don't know what
> Coptics believe and if they do, what on Earth makes
> them think they should be categorized as Christians.[7]

I didn't watch the entire video of these killings, but I did watch a "sanitized" version that showed these men kneeling in front of their captors, knowing they would soon die. One analyst reported, "As the blade came to their neck they all cried in unison, '*Ya Rabbi Yasou*' " or "O My Lord Jesus."[8]

An arrogant heart assumes what is in the heart of another, never having met or spoken with that person. Our only view into the lives of these Coptic Christians was what we saw moments before their deaths. We saw their peace, love for, and faith in Christ. They died for their faith singing, not begging, pleading, or crying—most certainly not denying Christ.

We are not all as arrogant in our misunderstanding as the critic quoted in the passage above. Yet most of us truly misunderstand much about our fellow Christians in other traditions. Charles Colson was not one of these individuals. He showed great clarity about other traditions without losing his evangelical convictions and passion.

Colson made his spiritual pilgrimage from Watergate conspirator to Prison Fellowship founder.[9] He journeyed from atheism to become a leader among evangelicals. Colson decried the "stubbornly held beliefs" "that one can't be a Christian if he or she is a Catholic" or "that one cannot be saved apart from the Catholic Church, despite Vatican II's clear words to the contrary."[10]

We misunderstand other traditions just as the churches in the East and the West misunderstood each other—the same way many still misunderstand the beliefs of Coptic Christians. Is it possible that misunderstandings that lasted a millennium and a half help to form the foundation of our lack of accord? Can we finally overcome our differences and misunderstandings for the sake of ministry? Some very notable Christians seem to think so.

Billy Graham began preaching in the 1940s. He and his evangelistic team decided early on that "emphasizing areas of agreement rather than disagreement with other clergy and Christian traditions" would help their young ministry avoid the snares that had taken down other revivalist efforts. Those dangers included "misuse of money, sexual immorality, exaggeration of results, and criticism of other clergy." Graham was willing "to work with almost anyone who would work with him as long as they did not ask him to change his message."[11]

His inclusive stance brought him flak from two different corners. He managed to irredeemably anger fundamentalists (the most conservative evangelicals) like Bob Jones. And many Catholics criticized Graham for his Protestant departures from "historic Christianity"—the papacy, the sacraments, and the "authority of tradition."[12] Graham felt opposition from those committed to separation, but he did not let them deter him from finding accord with many other Christians regardless of their faith tradition.

When it came to Graham's crusade meetings, Catholics had a notable presence. A demographic of attendees shows that Catholics ranked seventh after six evangelical and Protestant denominations. (He worked to make his meetings ethnically diverse as well.)[13]

Graham cultivated friendships with notable Catholic leaders such as Bishop Fulton J. Sheen and Richard John Cardinal Cushing. The criticism Graham's ministry received from Catholics in the early days of his ministry eventually dissolved into globally effective accord as we shall see later. But the rift between Graham and some fundamentalists lasted for decades. Some still rant against Graham on websites and in books.[14]

In spite of the critics, Billy's son Franklin has gone beyond his father's outreach by including Catholic believers as counselors for his events. Kristina M. DeNeve was a Catholic counselor for a BGEA (Billy Graham Evangelistic Association) festival (no longer called a crusade):

> At leadership meetings, pastors of other denominations often had spirited conversations with me about why Catholics were involved with this festival and whether or not they thought it was a good idea. Similarly, I participated in several sacred conversations with the BGEA festival director for Green Bay as well as with other individual Christians, grappling with an invisible line that moved from discomfort to full collaboration.

DeNeve was having the kinds of conversations that can lead to accord and allow Christians from all traditions to proclaim the gospel together.[15]

The church is a collection of people separated by various doctrines but joined in our love of Christ. Accord joins different colored glass pieces the way my parents were joined in marriage. Because of their difficulties, their life together wasn't a pristine picture of glee. But their faithfulness painted a picture of devotion and commitment—of pursuing right over desire and personal comfort. Imperfect pieces present the image of the Bride to the world. And cracked glass refracts more light.

Separation happens when authentic glass doesn't acknowledge other authentic glass of a different hue. Division happens when inauthentic glass rejects the essential doctrines of orthodoxy. Those doctrines are the foundation of accord. They prove the glass in the window is real.

Transfiguring Grace

Paradox:

To see my own sin—my own failings and imperfections—
To overlook yours.

Joy:

To have His grace wash over me and splash onto you,
To have His grace soak us both through,
And stain us forever with His love.

{ENDNOTES}

1   Victoria Finlay, "Why Colors You See in an Art Museum Can't Be Replicated Today," Smithsonian.com, November 14, 2014, https://www.smithsonianmag.com/arts-culture/why-colors-you-see-art-museum-cant-be-replicated-today-180953332.

2   Ware, *The Orthodox Church*, 212.

3   Ibid., 3–4.

4   Fr. Andrew Tevington, "Christian Coptic Church Arose from Oriental Orthodox Split in 451," *The Oklahoman*, February 23, 2008, http://newsok.com/article/3207549.

5   Ibid.

6   Daniel Burke, "In Historic Meeting, Pope and Russian Patriarch Issue Plea for Persecuted Christians," CNN, February 13, 2016, https://www.cnn.com/2016/02/12/europe/pope-francis-patriarch-kyril-meeting/index.html. See also Nicole Winfield, "Pope Francis Invites Orthodox Patriarch Bartholomew to Prayer Summit with Mahmoud Abbas and Shimon Peres," *Huffington Post,* June 4, 2014, https://www.huffingtonpost.com/2014/06/04/orthodox-patriarch-pope-abbas-peres_n_5440025.html.

7   *Pulpit and Pen*, "Coptic Christians Not Christians, Evangelical Leaders Need Reminded," February 16, 2015, http://pulpitandpen.org/2015/02/16/coptic-christians-not-christians-southern-baptist-leaders-need-reminded.

8   Stefan J. Bos, "21 Egypt Christians Praised Christ before Beheadings," Religious Freedom Coalition, February 19, 2015, https://www.religiousfreedomcoalition.org/2015/02/19/21-egypt-christians-praised-christ-before-beheadings.

9   Colson had become a Christian before he entered prison for his Watergate involvement. After his release, he began Prison Fellowship to minister to inmates and their families. See Prisonfellowship.org.

10   Charles Colson with Ellen Santilli Vaughn, *The Body: Being Light in Darkness* (Nashville: Word Publishing, 1992), 102.

11   Grant Wacker, *America's Pastor: Billy Graham and the Shaping of a Nation* (Cambridge: Belknap, 2014), 11, 29.

12   Ibid., 92.

13   Ibid., 253.

14 For example, see Christopher J. E. Johnson, "Wolves in Costume: Billy Graham," Creation, Liberty, Evangelism, July 17, 2013, http://www.creationliberty.com/articles/graham.php; Cathy Burns, *Billy Graham and His Friends: A Hidden Agenda?* (Sharing: 2006).

15 Kristina M. DeNeve, "Billy Graham Crusades and Catholic Evangelism," 21stcenturycatholicevangelization.org, vol. 24, no. 3 (May 2013), http://www.21stcenturycatholicevangelization.org/uploads/5/1/6/4/5164069/bill_graham_crusades__catholic_evangelization.pdf.

Five
REAL GLASS, FAKE GLASS

"But false prophets also arose among the people, just as there
will also be false teachers among you, who will secretly
introduce destructive heresies, even denying the Master who
bought them, bringing swift destruction upon themselves."

2 Peter 2:1

"As properly defined, stained glass is only that glass which has
been painted with special pigments and kiln fired to fuse the
pigments with the superficial layer of the glass."[1]

Claude Lips

The Holy Spirit colors his glass pieces with truth. Like well-crafted stained glass, truth won't break, and it can't fade either. Once the glass is fired, the color cannot become separate from the glass. Poorly crafted glass has color painted on, color that can rub off. That glass isn't real stained glass.

My earliest memories of church were in my mother's Methodist congregation, a neighborhood church so close we seldom drove there. The carpet and pew padding were crimson. Behind the pulpit, a portrait showed Christ praying in the garden of Gethsemane. It was here that my soul first absorbed a pigment of God's truth: He is, and he sees me.

When I was about to enter fourth grade, my father enrolled me in a local Catholic elementary school. The first Mass I remember was in Latin, but it was to be my last Latin Mass. That week, the small church building was razed, and the more modern, auditorium-like sanctuary was where I heard my first Mass in English.

One day, the priest introduced the topic of ecumenism. I don't recall him using that word. He seemed to be saying that we could talk with others—that it was somehow okay now, and it had not been before. He was really saying that we could pray with Christians of other traditions. We could address the almighty Creator of the universe together.

I didn't realize the significance then of having a father who was Catholic and a mother who was Methodist. I do now. My parents taught me to pray with no apparent conflict over "The Lord's Prayer" versus "Hail, Mary." We addressed the almighty Creator of the universe together every evening when we sat down to have dinner together.

One particular dinner in 1965 began as an ordinary, insignificant meal. I don't remember what we were eating, but our lives changed as we sat together. My oldest brother announced that he had enlisted in the navy earlier that day. My clearest memory that evening was Mother's fork clanking on her plate and her outcry of "What?!"

My brother had just earned an associate degree in electrical engineering from Penn State. America's involvement in Vietnam was growing, but he could have gotten a draft deferment merely by remaining in college. He could have earned a bachelor's degree in two years. Maybe the war would be over by then.

The separation of distance was about to change my family.

But the separation of ideas was what changed Christianity. Luther nailing his 95 Theses to the door of the All Saints Church in Wittenberg, Germany, in 1517 is the moment Chesterton named as Christianity's shattering point—our point of separation. Later, though, a philosophy would blossom and solidify a breach between conservative and liberal Christianity—our point of division.

Naturalism and evolution were not new ideas when Charles Darwin published his *Origin of Species* in 1859. Others had proposed that people were not creations of a divine order, that we had descended from other creatures. But in the nineteenth century, Darwin's ideas found a foothold along with the more encompassing notion that science, not theology, held the keys to the mysteries of the universe.

As Darwinian secularism gained popularity, conservative traditions remained committed to orthodoxy and were active in ministry—preaching the gospel and helping the poor. But not everyone who accepted Darwin's theory left the conservative fold.

A modern example is Francis S. Collins, who led the Genome Project, uncovering the intricacies of DNA and solving many puzzles of disease. Collins is a Christian who accepts much of Darwin's theory while rejecting the notion that science holds all the answers to life.

> God is at least, in part, outside of nature. Science has no ability to comment about things that are outside of nature. It's a categorical error to try to do so, and to use scientific argument to say *yes* or *no* to the existence of God is not a productive pathway ... . It requires a supreme amount of confidence to say, "I know there is no God." Suppose the knowledge of God's existence just happens to be outside of what you know at the moment.[2]

The distinction between separation and division over Darwin is not simply a debate over creation versus evolution. Our perspective on theology and science helps determine our beliefs, not only about human origin but also about human meaning and purpose and human destiny after death. These beliefs help shape whether we believe we are earthly, temporal agents who cease to exist at death or beings with a definite beginning (conception) who, after death, will continue to exist in heaven or hell perpetually.

If God created us, no matter how, we're here to fulfill his purposes. We're accountable to him—the One who, with intention, puts us here and gives us meaning. There can be no higher calling than to serve him. We can believe God made us and disagree over how he did so and still strive to follow him faithfully, appreciating the sacred meaning of our lives and pursuing his purpose for us. That God has shaped us and infused us with meaning, purpose, and destiny is the crucial point.

Many liberal churches, on the other hand, have adopted what Christian Smith calls Moralistic Therapeutic Deism—maintaining five points of doctrine:

> 1. "A god exists who created and ordered the world and watches over human life on earth." 2. "God wants people to be good, nice, and fair to each other, as taught in the Bible and by most world religions." 3. "The central goal of life is to be happy and to feel good about one's self." 4. "God does not need to be particularly involved in one's life except when God is needed to resolve a problem." 5. "Good people go to heaven when they die."[3]

In this realm of belief, orthodoxy has dissolved into a form of secularism with the mere trappings of Christianity. Liberal churches cling to a vague notion of a passive Jesus plus social action—the social gospel: good deeds and desacralized reason. Many conservative Christians who reject ecumenism do so in an effort to avoid joining themselves to such a philosophy. And rightly so.

Charles Colson described this kind of ecumenism as "the belief in nothing, save perhaps the fatherhood of God and the brotherhood of man."[4] This perspective has infiltrated denominations across the board. It proposes to improve the world without changing hearts. It can give people food but not hope. We must reject this view and offer to the needy both material assistance and the hope of the gospel. Unlike the easily visible separation between liturgical traditions and evangelicalism, this divide is prevalent today within nearly every Christian denomination—but often impossible to discern just through a denominational label.

Visit a random church on a random Sunday and you may find your preconceived notions about a particular denomination dashed. You may hear liberal philosophy where you expected orthodoxy, or you may hear orthodoxy where you least expected it. The wheat and the tares are indeed interwoven. It's a schism that's hidden within the folds of denominations. Many misconceptions we have about each other's traditions reside within this divide between orthodox and liberal thinking.

Liberal thought, apparent in the hierarchy of organizations such as the World Council of Churches and the National Council of Churches, has caused countless conservative evangelicals to reject ecumenism altogether. Many evangelicals see ecumenism as an effort to create one church—a crossless entity that rejects orthodoxy and promotes liberal goals. This fear is not without foundation. Early in the twentieth century, there was an effort to do exactly that.

The roots of the early liberal ecumenical movement were patently Protestant in nature. The organizers of the 1910 World Missionary Conference in Edinburgh, Scotland, failed to invite Catholics and Orthodox representatives. Among the conference planners was Charles Clayton Morrison.

From 1908 to 1947, Morrison was editor of *The Christian Century*—a magazine devoted to promoting unity among liberal Protestant denominations and minimizing Catholic influence in American society. Morrison headed an effort that would ultimately weaken the Christian underpinnings of our culture. And his efforts produced consequences he did not foresee.

In 1939, President Franklin Roosevelt appointed a "personal representative" (rather than an official ambassador representing the US) to the Vatican. In response, Morrison helped found Protestants and Other Americans United for the Separation of Church and State (POAU). The organization was a "patriotic" group determined to preserve "religious liberty"—Protestant liberty—and to further marginalize Catholicism. After World War II, the group was larger than its pre-war counterpart. It included representatives from major mainline denominations, the Federal Council of Churches (later the National Council of Churches), and the World Council of Churches. Sadly, the National Association of Evangelicals also joined the POAU effort.[5]

Those involved had one goal: they "wanted their church to function as the national church" of America—the symbolic spiritual guide for our country.[6] That "church," however, never developed into the one worldwide, doctrinally indistinct church that evangelicals feared, for it never materialized.

Morrison's hope to establish a national Protestant church, if only symbolically, smacks more of anti-Catholic bias and less of biblical evangelism. At the time, Morrison and his associates perceived that two entities threatened the hope of a national American Protestant church. One was the Catholic Church; the other was secularism. POAU fought on both fronts.

In 1947, the US Supreme Court ruled that states could use tax dollars to transport students to Catholic schools. And in 1948, the court ruled that public schools could no longer provide religious instruction. In this context, POAU found itself arguing out of both sides of its mouth. On the one hand, it argued that limiting religious instruction in public schools restricted the free exercise of religion. On the other hand, it asserted that tax dollars for Catholic schoolchildren's transportation comprised an unconstitutional establishment of a government religion. And that establishment of religion violated an alleged separation of church and state.[7]

Secularists have carried the banner of separation of church and state ever since.

But the liberal perspective wasn't the only one seeking some form of harmony among various denominations. While liberal ecumenism worked to undermine Catholicism, a different and more inclusive effort arose. Some conservative Protestants proposed accord with Catholics.

Lutheran pastor and key player in the German resistance effort during World War II, Dietrich Bonhoeffer was "extremely pro-Catholic and [acknowledged that] much of his own theology was specifically formed by Catholicism."[8] Bonhoeffer was influenced by a conservative ecumenism that Karl Barth also promoted, and Bonhoeffer was thoroughly orthodox in his theology.[9]

Barth himself had come to realize that his view "agrees with the Roman Catholic view (of salvation); if only for the reason that the Roman Catholic teaching would then be most strikingly in accord with mine!" Barth realized that he had "been guilty of a thoroughgoing misunderstanding and, consequently, of a thoroughgoing injustice regarding the teaching of [the Catholic] Church, especially that of the Fathers of Trent"—those who developed the Catholic response to Luther.[10]

But Barth wasn't Bonhoeffer's only influence. During his first trip to America, Bonhoeffer witnessed a profound display of faith in a Harlem church.

> [W]hat Bonhoeffer saw was a huge congregation of African-Americans who took their faith seriously. They were a people who weren't merely playing at religion. Many of the older people in that congregation had been born during slavery times; so they were not strangers to suffering, and their faith was obviously real.
>
> ... He got very involved in the lives of the people [there], and it changed his life. There's little question about that.[11]

Bonhoeffer wanted to carry the message of conservative ecumenism—accord in orthodoxy—to the next generation. And he worked toward this end until the Nazis executed him shortly before Germany surrendered, silencing a voice who may have helped us overcome our separation.

In the years following World War II, the divide between the liberal and conservative wings of Christianity would only expand, and the acceptance of less than orthodox theology would cause the liberal side of modern Christianity to shrink.

As *New York Times* columnist Ross Douthat explains, in the sixties and seventies, much of America signed on for moral relativism and redistribution that liberal churches promoted. But along the way, they lost their connection to a church community.

> Any institution that calls human beings to devotion and self-sacrifice needs to justify that call. The accommodationist [liberal] churches had no such institutional justification—or at least, they had no justification that explained why Americans should be involved with their church *in particular* [Douthat's emphasis] ... . Why would you need to wash down your left-wing convictions with a draft of Communion wine, when you could take the activism straight and do something else with your weekends?[12]

Leading Catholic authority George Weigel agrees that liberal theology is unable "to transmit the faith to successor generations." Liberal claims were "watering down ... Catholic truth claims [orthodoxy]." And this inability to transmit the faith "has now been amply demonstrated throughout the religious wasteland of Western Europe, the part of the world Church that adopted the progressive project most enthusiastically."[13]

My father and our family's priest found themselves on opposite ends of this discussion. The priest expressed two views that ended our family's faithful attendance at Mass. He stated that the Bible stories were "fairy tales," and he preached against America's involvement in the Vietnam War.

Dad didn't tell me at the time why we stopped going to church. Years later when he did explain, he didn't have to say why he found both of the priest's ideas unconscionable. He had been disappointed to see English replace Latin in the Mass, but discrediting the Bible from the pulpit was just too much. To top that off with political comments about a war when this World War II navy veteran had a son in uniform pushed him completely out the parish's door.

Our family's experience with the liberal side of Catholic tradition didn't mean that liberal thought had completely overtaken Catholicism. Another Catholic perspective was more in line with Dad's thinking—the traditionalist view. This faction rejected Vatican II and all the changes it brought as a "terribly-mistaken-concession-to-modernity."[14]

Still, there was a third perspective in this discussion. Another voice, more authoritative, spoke within Catholicism. It illustrates the unseen schism that separates us without regard to denomination. Rejecting both the liberal/progressive view and the traditionalist view, Weigel says the Church presents a third option: evangelical Catholicism. Evangelical Catholicism does not adopt "modes of worship from evangelical ... Protestantism."[15] But it "is a friendship with the Lord Jesus Christ ... . Evangelical Catholicism begins not with *knowing about* Jesus, but with *knowing* Jesus."[16] Weigel credits Pope John Paul II (now Saint John Paul II), aided by Cardinal Joseph Ratzinger (later Pope Benedict XVI), with putting "evangelical heart and courage back into the Catholic Church."[17]

Here we see the true schism within Catholicism—the liberal side, which rejects orthodoxy, and the "evangelical" side, which encourages relationship with Christ. This division also exists within Methodism, Presbyterianism, Anglicanism, and numerous other denominations. And while it is harder to see than denominational separation, we can see its effects in our communities. One time vibrant neighborhood ministry sites are now abandoned buildings. Organizations that had once held high the evangelical banner but took up liberal (or no) theology, the YMCA and YWCA for example, became secularized shadows of their noble past—a past that evolved from the true gospel to the social gospel and then to no gospel. That's where the social gospel will always lead—to no gospel.

The social gospel is cheap glass. The world sees that it is not real and rejects it. But as the liberal side of Christendom moved away from orthodoxy, the conservative side, the evangelical portion of it at least, also moved. It moved *away* from ministry. The true gospel is real glass, but Christians at a distance from ministry block the light.

The Cold Within

Six humans trapped by happenstance
In black and bitter cold.
Each one possessed a stick of wood,
Or so the story's told.

Their dying fire in need of logs,
The first woman held hers back
For on the faces around the fire,
She noticed one was black.

The next man looking cross the way
Saw one not of his church,
And couldn't bring himself to give
The fire his stick of birch.

The third man sat in tattered clothes;
He gave his coat a hitch.
Why should his log be put to use
To warm the idle rich?

The rich man just sat back and thought
Of the wealth he had in store.
And how to keep what he had earned
From the lazy poor.

The black man's face bespoke revenge
As the fire passed from his sight,

For all he saw in his stick of wood
Was a chance to spite the white.

And the last man of this forlorn group
Did naught except for gain.
Giving only to those who gave
Was how he played the game.

The logs held tight in death's still hands
Was proof of human sin.
They didn't die from the cold without,
They died from the cold within.[18]

JAMES PATRICK KINNEY

{Endnotes}

1   Lips, *Art and Stained Glass,* 10.

2   Francis S. Collins, "The Language of God: A Believer Looks at the Human Genome," in Eric Metaxas, ed., *Life, God, and Other Small Topics: Conversations from Socrates in the City* (New York: Penguin Books, 2011), 314.

3   Albert Mohler, "Moralistic Therapeutic Deism—the New American Religion," April 10, 2005, https://albertmohler.com/2005/04/11/moralistic-therapeutic-deism-the-new-american-religion-2.

4   Colson, *The Body,* 97. Colson uses terms from Henry Ward Beecher that proposed just such a form of ecumenism.

5   Elesha J. Coffman, *"The Christian Century" and the Rise of the Protestant Mainline* (Oxford: Oxford University Press, 2013), 158.

6   Ibid., 159–60.

7   Ibid.

8   *Catholic News Agency,* "Author Calls Dietrich Bonhoeffer a Man of 'Staggering' Relevance for Our Time,"July 25, 2010, https://www.catholicnewsagency.com/news/author-calls-dietrich-bonhoeffer-a-man-of-staggering-relevance-for-our-time.

9   Eric Metaxas, *Bonhoeffer: Pastor, Martyr, Prophet, Spy* (Nashville: Thomas Nelson, 2010), 61.

10   Karl Barth, "A Letter to the Author," in Hans Küng, *Justification* (Louisville: Westminster John Knox Press, 2004), lxvii-lxviii, as quoted in "Karl Barth and Roman Catholicism via Hans Kung," *Theo Philogue,* accessed July 31, 2014, https://theophilogue.com/2009/04/08/karl-barth-and-roman-catholicism-via-hans-kung.

11   Eric Metaxas, "How Good Confronts Evil," in Metaxas, *Life, God, and Other Small Matters,* 339–40.

12   Ross Douthat, *Bad Religion: How We Became a Nation of Heretics* (New York: Free Press, 2012), 108–109.

13   Weigel, *Evangelical Catholicism,* 17.

14   Ibid., 15.

15   Ibid., 3.

16   Ibid., 56–57, Weigel's emphasis.

17   Ibid., 10.

18   James Patrick Kinney, "The Cold Within," c. 1960.

Six
THE LOOKING GLASS

"For if anyone is a hearer of the word and not a doer,
he is like a man who looks at his natural face
in a mirror; for once he has looked at himself and gone away,
he has immediately forgotten what kind of person he was."

JAMES 1:23–24

"A group of MIT scientists have created a new material that can be
both a mirror and a window, and no it's not a one-way mirror.
This new material can filter light depending on the direction of the light
beams … . [L]ight that hits from one angle goes straight through … but
light that hits the material at different angles is reflected back."[1]

CHRISTIE NICHOLSON

Through the stained glass window of the church we see the light that God emits, the light that he is. We cannot see him directly, but we begin to understand who he is—his nature and characteristics. We see his holiness.

With a change in the angle of the light, we see our own reflection—our hearts in the light of his holiness. We see cracks and dirt, and we know we can't fix ourselves.

After our family stopped attending Mass, there was a void in my spiritual journey. Yet God had sowed seeds of understanding in my heart through my Methodist and Catholic experiences. We didn't attend church, but I was sure of God—certain he was aware of me and aware of all I thought and did. I had few moments of doubt, though I prayed for assurance of his acceptance of me.

When I moved from junior high to high school, I met a new set of friends. Some of them understood the need to know and follow Christ.

In the early seventies, at the urging of a family friend, I attended an evangelistic meeting and received Christ. I had glimpsed into a looking glass, and I saw the twisted glass of me. Only Christ could reshape me. I had never heard this message before. I knew I had sinned, but I had not understood the need to commit my life to Christ. There was much I still didn't understand. More interested in escaping hell than following a challenging path, I thought I had eternity to gain and nothing to lose. There seemed to be no cost to count.

I began to attend a small church where a couple of friends encouraged me. But there was no one I could confide in, no youth group, no mentors, not the kind of discipleship a young girl would need in the wake of the sexual revolution. I dressed up and put on my perfect mask to go to church. The mask told everyone that I had it all together—no moral questions, no problems, no wounds from the past that might take me off course. I had turned onto a new path. But my walk was superficial. My faith was two inches deep.

I broke up with my boyfriend whose beliefs differed from mine, but several months later, I was dating a new guy. Convictions inhabited my head, but an idol had my heart. At key turning points, I picked my boyfriend, not my Lord, and strayed.

A shallow walk impresses others for a time, but it skewed my own reflection. Soon I was a girl in trouble. As expectant teens, my boyfriend and I married. I would pay for leaving the path—not the cost of discipleship but the price of sin.

In the twentieth century, Christianity in America continued along two separate paths. As it should have, the rift between liberal and conservative theology widened. But both sides had strayed from preaching the gospel and helping the poor. Both sides had moved.

The liberal side departed from the truth of the gospel, and the conservative side, at least part of it, backed away from assisting the needy. "As evangelicals tried to distance themselves from the social gospel movement, they ended up in large-scale retreat from the front lines of poverty alleviation."[2] Evangelicals stopped caring for their neighbors to avoid the appearance of endorsing the social gospel.

However, evangelicals didn't withdraw from meeting needs altogether. For some time, evangelical mission efforts remained robust. Joe Dillon, a missional church strategist for the International Mission Board, explains that Depression era missions zeal eclipses our current American missionary efforts: "Even during the Great Depression, when unemployment stood at 35 percent, American churches gave proportionately three times to international missions what churches of today give. During those earlier times ... churches would forgo buying coal to heat their buildings so that the money could instead be used to keep missionaries on the field."[3] Christians chose discomfort rather than allowing the mission effort to wane. As they sacrificed to keep missions going, churches passed resources over the heads of their needy neighbors. Even so, individuals still steeped in a Judeo-Christian ethic fed neighbors and strangers in need. It was common for "hobos" to knock on doors and request a meal. It was uncommon for anyone to turn them away empty handed.

As economic conditions improved in the next decade and beyond, the face of poverty in America became less well known to those in even relative affluence. With abundance around us and the stigma of the social gospel lurking, we became skeptical of those in need. Today's hobos, the homeless, know better than to knock on many of our doors and ask us for food.

The shift away from one form of church ministry—namely, local assistance—would eventually result in diminished mission support. We no longer interacted with our needy neighbors. And we saw the faces of the mission field projected on a screen just a few times a year.

Since the days of self-deprivation to send the gospel abroad, foreign mission giving and efforts have declined proportionally.[4] By the early part of the twenty-first century, only "one-tenth of one percent (ten cents per hundred dollars) of all Christian income went to global foreign missions."[5]

Having spurned our local needy and reduced our mission support, there is no one else left for us to minister to but ourselves. Our centrally heated, opulent worship centers, no longer sanctuaries, tell the tale. Using the term *worship center* puts the focus on us—the activity we are engaging in. Its focus is inward. On the other hand, a *sanctuary* implies an outward focus. A sanctuary is open to everyone, especially to the transgressor.

God told Moses to establish six sanctuary cities ("cities of refuge")— havens for anyone who had accidentally killed someone.[6] The concept of churches providing sanctuary to those who had run afoul of the law or the king lasted for centuries in Europe. The shift in our usage from *sanctuary* to *worship center* accurately reflects the shift from outreach to self-fulfillment.

Meanwhile, need is all around us. Broken people need personal investment, not only material provision, but compassion and time, the spiritual factors that government can't contribute. Broken people need mentors to guide them to stability and independence. They need discipleship to guide them to the right path—the path of depth rather than superficiality.

My community of companions from various Christian traditions encouraged me in my quest for a college degree. They not only told me that I could succeed, many of them also took the time to help me know *how* to succeed. And they did so without making me feel pitied or patronized. As they pointed the way, they showed me their own depth of faith through which they discipled me. They showed me *imago Dei*—the image of God—and a clear picture of who I am as part of his picture.

The active, living church is the glass that displays the image of God's grace. But some have never even seen it.

We tend to think that those who have not heard the good news live on remote shores. But 20 percent of North American non-Christians do not even know a Christian. Nearly 13.5 million people on our continent have no personal context to gauge the body of Christ.[7] "Eighty-seven percent of 18- to 35-year-olds who are outside the church think the church is judgmental ... . [M]ost of the world sees Jesus as being full of grace while his followers are full of judgment."[8]

Along with seeing us as judgmental, those who don't know us often see us as hypocrites. In fairness, those outside the church have many reasons to believe Christians are self-righteous and insincere. One reason is that the media seldom present true Christianity. How can someone whose only example of Christianity is a cartoonish sitcom character or an angry protester on a newscast ever develop a positive impression of our faith? There are also the charlatans who dance across our television screens promising God's favor in exchange for cash donations—the parallel to medieval indulgences. In light of such misrepresentations and in the absence of any contact with actual Christians, it's no wonder that non-Christians cannot see true Christianity through the cloud of masquerading frauds.

And sometimes the world perceives us as judgmental because we are. Sometimes "loving the sinner and hating the sin" are empty words we use to justify our disapproval of people in whose shoes we have not walked and whose stories we do not know—people just like the ones Christ taught, healed, and forgave.

We also judge other Christians whose traditions don't match ours. In the same way non-Christians misrepresent our faith, we often misrepresent other Christian traditions. Just as with the Monophysite schism between the Oriental Orthodox and Greek and Latin Christians that occurred five hundred years after Christ, what we think we know may be a distortion—*our* distortion of *their* faith. And what others think they know about us may be skewed as well.

The accusation of easy believism is one basis for a distortion of evangelical Christianity. Some in the liturgical community view evangelical conversion as a sort of enrollment in a club that involves no sacrifice, no works, just membership. It does not clear up the confusion when evangelical leaders tell their congregations, "It doesn't matter what you do after you are saved." Many within evangelical circles understand this statement to mean that eternal life is God's gift through grace and no one can earn heaven through good works. Most evangelicals realize Christianity requires sacrifice and obedience. If they haven't learned it yet, they soon will, as I did. However, what those outside evangelical circles may hear is the opposite—that evangelical faith is easy and does not require daily dying to self. Some churches falsely offer an easy gospel. But what they present is distortion rather than true biblical faith. People coming to Christ need to hear that faith has a cost and sin has a price—even in a free society. True Christian faith, no matter the tradition, requires obedience and sacrifice. A person who claims to be a Christian but refuses to be obedient and does not experience conviction of sin is no true follower of Christ.

But distortion is not a one-way street. A common distortion by the evangelical side is that Catholics and Christian Orthodox engage in Mary worship. Official Catholic teaching states that while Catholics are to "honor" Mary, this devotion "differs essentially from the adoration which is given to the incarnate Word [Jesus] and equally to the Father and the Holy Spirit."[9] Eastern Orthodoxy also venerates Mary, making the same distinction between veneration and worship.[10] If we disagree with the veneration of Mary, we have an authentic disagreement. But to say that this veneration is worship presents a distortion of the doctrine.

Catholicism itself works to ensure that veneration of Mary is appropriate and does not cross into the realm of worship. Catholic author Colleen Carroll Campbell points to passages from Vatican II decrying "excesses of Marian devotion [that] could distract from Christ and confuse non-Catholics." These excesses may be what evangelicals are pointing to as they criticize "Mary worship." Campbell admits that she has encountered "Catholics who succumbed to such excesses" but that actual Church teaching promotes a "genuine affection, admiration, and a desire to imitate [Mary's] virtues." This correct form of devotion would "always lead [Catholics] closer to Christ and [help them] remain rooted in Christ ... 'the source of all truth, sanctity, and devotion.' "[11]

Presenting this distortion from the pulpit, in the classroom, or in general conversation has power. It can lead some Catholics to cross a line into worship. But doing so distorts their faith. At the same time, some evangelicals can fall into the trap of easy believism. And this distorts their faith.

It's wrong to judge Catholicism on the basis of Mary "worship" just as it's wrong to judge evangelicalism by the prosperity gospel of ease and comfort. To do so is akin to judging fundamentalist Christians because of a few snake handlers. Or judging Baptist Christians on the basis of the Westboro Baptist Church, a "church" that picketed military funerals with signs proclaiming that "God hates fags."

Such distortions present faith as a straw man argument—finding a perspective's weakest point, changing it or exaggerating it in some way, and then presenting it as foundational fact. Attacking any position with such a tactic makes the position seem weak, silly, and sometimes even absurd. This technique makes it easy to knock down someone's faith perspective. But it's a straw man fallacy in reasoning, and it's not the way we should treat one another in the family of God (or even outside of the family for that matter). We can disagree with one another once we genuinely understand one another's view. But it's not right to misrepresent anyone's faith.

We won't fix every misperception people have that we are a judgmental people, but we can work to understand each other in accord. To do so brings the image of the window into focus for everyone. As Christ promised, some people will always hate us. We have to ask ourselves whether they will hate us because we lack compassion or in spite of our abundant love.

The mirror shows our true selves; it lets us see our own sin as well as our forgiven state. We can see ourselves as sinners and as sacred beings whom God loves. As long as we are alive, that image will be changing. The image transforms as God uses our experiences to shape us into better conveyors of his love.

Being a Christian is about gazing at the God in whose image you were made and, in love, reflecting that image out into the world.[12]

N. T. WRIGHT

{ENDNOTES}

1   Christie Nicholson, "A Material That Can Be a Mirror, Then a Window," Core 77, April 16, 2014, http://www.core77.com/posts/26791/a-material-that-can-be-a-mirror-then-a-window-26791.

2   Steve Corbett and Brian Fikkert, *When Helping Hurts: How to Alleviate Poverty without Hurting the Poor and Yourself* (Chicago: Moody Press, 2012), 44.

3   Mike Creswell, "US Missionary Sending in Decline, IMB Strategist Says," BRnow.org, March 26, 2013, https://brnow.org/News/March-2013/U-S-missionary-sending-in-decline-IMB-strategist.

4   Ibid.

5   David Barrett, "Status of Global Mission" (2005), as quoted by Jim Sutherland, "The Western Church and Global Missions Giving: A Case for Discernment," Giving and Missions, 2013, accessed October 9, 2013, https://www.rmni.org/files/financial/Giving%20and%20Missions.pdf.

6   Numbers 35:10–15.

7   See Abby Stocker, "The Craziest Statistic You'll Read about North American Missions," *Christianity Today*, August 19, 2013.

8   Tim Harlow, "Sticky Conversations: Alcohol," *Christian Standard*, October 15, 2012, http://harlow51.rssing.com/browser.php?indx=16919203&item=3.

9   *Catechism of the Catholic Church* (New Hope, KY: Urbi et Orbi Communications, 1994), 971.

10 See Fr. Dn. Charles Joiner, "Ten Things Orthodox Christians Would Like You to Know," *Orthodox Way of Life*, February 17, 2014, http://orthodoxwayoflife.blogspot.com/2014/02/10-things-orthodox-christians-would.html.

11 Colleen Carroll Campbell, *My Sisters the Saints: A Spiritual Memoir* (New York: Image, 2012), 185–86.

12 N. T. Wright, "Simply Christian: Why Christianity Makes Sense," in Metaxas, *Life, God, and Other Small Topics*, 216.

Seven
CONSTANT LIGHT, SHIFTING SAND

*"I will make you a light for the nations, And You will illumine
them until My salvation reaches to the ends of the earth."*

ISAIAH 49:6 THE VOICE

*"In the course of the day [stained glass windows] are animated
by changing light, their patterns wandering across the floor,
inviting your thoughts to wander with them. They were essential
to the fabric of ancient churches, illuminating the building
and the people within, both literally and spiritually."*[1]

ANDY CONNELLY

My firstborn, Angela Marie, arrived after thirty-six hours of labor, weighing six pounds and eleven ounces. New life in my arms beckoned me to move closer to God. I brought her home from the hospital on my nineteenth birthday. Life was now a new place where she and I would both grow up.

But drawing closer to God painted my sin like a big neon sign in my heart. This blinding neon light obscured the soothing glow of the window. My assurance had vanished. Because I had chosen my way instead of God's will, I questioned the validity of my commitment to Christ. My life didn't match the picture of the window.

Now I wanted to be a good Christian, to set a good example for my child. I stumbled along at this point, forming convictions, often legalistic ones. I wavered between distrust and untested trust, and lived by rules. The rules were the yardstick I used to measure the faith of others—the means by which I established my righteousness. I was a dull and dusty piece of glass.

Over the next few years, our little family moved from an apartment to a trailer, I quit my job, and we welcomed our son, Mike. But the trailer was crowded, so we found a frame house on a hill to turn into home. Cordial neighbors welcomed us. As the children grew, their community of playmates increased. And the playground of backyards soon expanded to include nearby woods for them to roam on long summer days.

Our community of friends was growing at church too, but my husband's job interfered with church attendance. He worked irregular hours, including Sundays, and slept while we were awake. Angela loved the friends she found at church, and as long as one particular woman was working in the nursery, Mike was happy.

Adversity seemed far from us in those days. But our house on the hill held a marriage on shifting sand. Had our days continued to glide along smoothly, my faith may have done the same. Soon, however, life became uncertain and more difficult. Through those times, my house on the Rock, my faith, became solid protection against the storms. The light of God's faithfulness overcame my neon guilt. I found that my suffering had a purpose. It led me to my place in the image of the window. As our commitment to Christ deepens, that image becomes clearer for us and for others. Suffering often leads to great clarity.

There are different kinds of suffering. There is the kind we inflict upon ourselves through poor choices. There is suffering by apparent chance—illness or accident. And there is suffering because of oppression and injustice. That kind of suffering may be the most clarifying of all.

In 1978, Cardinal Karol Wojtyla became Pope John Paul II, the first non-Italian pope in 456 years. Not only was he not Italian; he was from Poland, a country where the government despised the Church. This new pope was different. Younger than any other pope in the previous century, he had survived the Nazi occupation only to endure Soviet oppression. He knew the suffering that is oppression, and it infused his ministry with vivid colors.

When Wojtyla was in Rome becoming the new pope, Billy Graham was in Poland preaching from Wojtyla's pulpit, having come at Wojtyla's invitation. No other Polish Catholic leader would agree to invite Graham, and he couldn't go without an invitation. Graham would later preach in Orthodox and Reformed churches, a Jewish synagogue, and an Orthodox monastery during his European travels.[2]

Wojtyla and Graham had planned to get together during Graham's visit, but Wojtyla's call to Rome for the papal election delayed their meeting.[3] Before Graham's arrival, Wojtyla had been overseeing a "radical partnership" between a Catholic youth renewal movement and Campus Crusade for Christ.[4] His work to light local flames of faith in the young kindled a global bonfire he could never have imagined.

In 1979, the new pope returned to his homeland where more than one million Poles lined the streets to welcome him and millions more came to hear him.[5] Lech Walesa, firebrand of the Solidarity movement in Poland, told Peggy Noonan in 2002 that "we knew the minute [John

Paul] touched the foundations of communism, it would collapse." Walesa credited "heaven and the Holy Father" as most responsible for destroying communism in Poland.[6]

The pope's visit to Poland was a tiny pebble dropped into a steaming pond. The resulting ripples turned into a tidal wave. When Mikhail Gorbachev became the Soviet premier, he saw the handwriting on the wall in Poland and began to implement reforms across the Soviet Union. He hoped to save communism by reforming it.[7]

But by then, the cracks in the foundation of communism were too deep. Ten years after the pope's return to his homeland in 1979, the Berlin Wall fell along with the Iron Curtain. The ripples of reform and freedom in Eastern Europe would reverberate across the globe.

Nineteen-eighty-nine was also the year Hu Yaobang died in China. Hu was a high-ranking communist official in the People's Republic. He had fallen out of favor with party power brokers because he supported reforms, loosening controls on the press and the people. Inspired by student protests in America and South Korea they had seen on television, Chinese college students gathered in Beijing at Tiananmen Square to mourn Hu, their advocate for democratic reform. The marathon sit-in lasted seven weeks. Demonstrations weren't unheard of in China, but the international broadcast of such demonstrations was. The international press was in town to cover Gorbachev's visit to Beijing. Because of his attempts to reform communism, the protesting Chinese students considered him a champion of democracy.[8] The presence of the international press made possible our knowledge of the Tiananmen Square massacre. In front of the international media, the Chinese government, having lost face in the weeks' long standoff, sent the army into the square, killing thousands and capturing surviving protesters.

Eastern European Christians would ultimately see freedom. The Chinese students, on the other hand, did not get the change they had hoped for, but change is what China would see. The Beijing massacre and imprisonment of surviving demonstrators prompted Chinese youth, especially students, to look for a new form of freedom. Many found that freedom in Christ. Why did young Chinese college students suddenly develop a passionate interest in the Christian faith? David Aikman writes that one "suggestion was that China's traditional Confucian view of man as inherently good was shattered under the tanks that rolled onto the center of Beijing."[9] The Chinese students had put their faith in their government, and their government turned on them and attacked them. Now they would look elsewhere for someone to trust. Within the next ten to fifteen years, China is on track to become the most Christian nation in the world.[10] The new wave of freedom that started in Catholic Poland ultimately sparked an explosion of evangelical Christianity halfway around the world. Pope John Paul II helped ignite that spark.

John Paul II began his papacy by hoping to visit his Catholic homeland. A faithful prayer warrior, he no doubt prayed for the people of his native land. The echoes of his first trek to Poland resonate around the world and into eternity. Christianity and the call for freedom have gone hand in hand throughout history because Christianity is the truest form of freedom. It frees us from the bonds of sin and points us to eternal concerns and away from irrelevant earthly ones.

The more freedom and opportunity we have, the more God expects of us, but it seems that the more personal comfort we have, the less we do for each other. In America's large cities, our neighborhoods are more alienated than ever. Fear, anger, and misunderstanding separate us. Many of us feed a selfishness that wants to gain comfort others already have. Some of us just want to hang on to our own level of comfort.

Historically, as Christianity emerges in a hostile society, Christians have come together to further the gospel. Pope, now Saint, John Paul II and Billy Graham showed us the difference accord can make in oppressed nations like Poland once was. But accord is also apparent in oppressed China.

I had the blessing of meeting one of the Chinese student protesters who turned to Christ after Tiananmen Square. I asked him about separation within the Chinese church. "Denomination is not important in China," was his reply.

As in Korea, America's Christian denominations are growing, if they are growing at all, by recruiting members of other traditions. Different traditions trade members, but seldom do those who grew up outside a Christian tradition come through the doors of faith.

Many notable Christian leaders of various denominations have found new homes in different traditions. Author Eric Metaxas left Greek Orthodoxy to find his evangelical home.[11] Wilbur Ellsworth preached at a Baptist church near Wheaton College before becoming a priest and leading a congregation largely comprised of fellow evangelical converts to Eastern Orthodoxy.[12] Lyle Dorsett was a Lutheran as a child, a Baptist as a teen, a prodigal in college, and is now an Anglican pastor in his adulthood. Dorsett quotes Peter C. Moore's "Anglican watchwords ... unity, diversity, and charity: unity in essentials [orthodoxy], diversity in nonessentials, and charity in all things.'"[13]

Finding those who've changed traditions is easy today. Forty-two percent of Americans have moved to a different denomination from the one where they grew up.[14] Ten percent of Americans are former Catholics. And nearly half of those who leave the Catholic Church become Protestant.[15] But the exodus is not a one-way street. Former evangelicals are "joining Catholic, Eastern Orthodox, or Anglican churches," all liturgical traditions.[16] Catholics are moving to evangelicalism as evangelicals are moving to Catholicism or Orthodoxy. Catholic writer Colleen Carroll explains why:

> American Catholicism [was] hemorrhag[ing those] who found Catholic worship lifeless and Catholics themselves unenthusiastic about the faith. Many gravitated to evangelical Christianity, which stresses the personal relationship with Christ that so many young Catholics seek.
>
> While many Catholics leave the church in search of a personal relationship with Christ and wind up in evangelical churches, converts to Catholicism bring with them the features of evangelicalism they loved about their childhood churches ... . Young converts who embrace Catholicism are often attracted by its emphasis on exactly those elements that drove their baby boomer parents away [from the Catholic Church]: its structure, liturgy, strict moral teachings, and tradition.[17]

Serious seekers who leave evangelicalism to pursue liturgical traditions are rejecting the easy believism and cheap grace philosophies that have infiltrated many churches. Serious seekers who leave Catholicism to become evangelicals are yearning for a deeper connection to God than they experienced in their native churches. Some are stolen sheep. Others are found sheep who wandered in search of a plush pasture of faith.

The diverse foundation of my youth helped me find the pasture of evangelicalism that has fed me so well for decades. The roots evangelicalism planted in my son's heart prepared him to find his home in Catholicism.

When I told some of my friends that my son, Chris, was considering Catholicism, I got various reactions. Of course, my Catholic friends were delighted (and gracious). Some of my evangelical friends were horrified—

as if he had turned to the Dark Side. A few assumed he converted, not out of personal conviction, but only, they imagined, because he had married a Catholic woman. (But his wife, Tyne, had actually grown up in the Lutheran Church.) Several responded positively, acknowledging his prayerful search for truth and celebrating his desire to follow Christ earnestly and with intention. Paula, one of my Bible study friends, was one who responded positively to this news. One of her sons had also become Catholic. She celebrated her son's decision as she comforted another friend who was upset at her own son leaving his Catholic tradition to become an evangelical.

In the spirit of full disclosure, my own reaction about Chris' conversion was mixed at first. I had been praying for God to give Chris and Tyne a church home. They had tried our church as well as her church. Neither one was a good fit for them as a couple, so for some time they did not attend church at all.

Chris had been a college student when his Army Reserve unit deployed to Iraq. When he returned, he switched majors and schools. At Mount Aloysius College, aside from his studies in accounting, he took a course on Catholicism and found it "fascinating."

After Chris and Tyne married, they began to attend Mass and take classes to prepare them to become members of the Church. Those pursuing membership in the Catholic Church have sponsors. Chris and Tyne's sponsors were Rick and Patsy who had also been evangelicals attending the same church we did years earlier.

I was surprised to learn that Chris and Tyne would not need to be baptized. And they did not need to get married again in their new church home. The Catholic Church recognized the baptisms and wedding they participated in as Protestants.

I learned other lessons too. Ideas that had been distortions of Catholic belief came into clearer focus. Partway through their months of study and several weeks before Easter, Chris and Tyne invited me to the Mass in which the Church would welcome them into fellowship. At this Mass, they would indicate their intention to become members of the Church. As part of his message that day, the priest asked those in the congregation to "Give your lives to God." I didn't think he could say anything more evangelical than that. My son and his wife were devoting themselves to God in a way that I had hoped and prayed they would, even if I had not imagined the form such devotion would take. Later, Chris told me about an earlier Mass when the priest told his flock, "the Church is your home. You are home when you are here." Here was the "home church" I had prayed they would find.

When Cardinal Wojtyla invited Billy Graham to preach, Catholicism largely *was* Christianity in Poland. While Polish Baptists had worked for twelve years to get Graham to their homeland, it was the Catholic Wojtyla who succeeded.[18] Wojtyla's goal was not to invite Polish Catholics to leave Catholicism but to invite them into relationship with God *within* their Catholic faith. In English and Polish, Graham and Wojtyla shared the language of Christian faith.

Many Christians who support accord propose that God enjoys diversity of tradition in his people. Instead, we might consider that we are the ones who need this diversity. Where he is infinite, we are narrow and small. Perhaps all of our denominational diversity is both grace and challenge. Grace is his love for those faithful to him regardless of tradition. The challenge is for us to love one another even when we disagree.

Perhaps Christ let us hear his garden prayer for our oneness, not because it would be easy, but because He knew it would be hard. He prayed and ensured through his Word that we would know his prayer. Accord is primarily love—caring more about the other person than about winning our nonessential point.

Hasty assumptions and misguided distortions contribute to resentment and separation. We should not object when one of our nominal members becomes a serious member of another Christian tradition. Such unity would shine light to the unchurched who reject Christ because they see our resentment and not our love. Jesus said, "I am the door; if anyone enters through Me, he will be saved, and will go in and out and find pasture."[19]

Jesus is the door; we are the window that shows the way to the door. God is the constant light that shines through his image of the window, the church. He brings those standing on shifting sand out of the darkness and onto solid ground.

Help Along the Way

Road ruts and briar bushes trip and ensnare.
Bruised and scratched,
Mother and children grope forward toward Zion.
Some urge them the wrong way.
Others walk with them,
Guiding their direction,
Reflecting his Light,
Showing them green pastures.

{Endnotes}

1   Andy Connelly, "Heavenly Illumination: The Science and Magic of Stained Glass," *The Guardian,* October 29, 2010, https://www.theguardian.com/science/blog/2010/oct/29/science-magic-stained-glass.

2   Wacker, *America's Pastor,* 203.

3   The pope would later visit with Graham in Rome multiple times, and the two corresponded through letters. When John Paul died, Graham said this pope had been the "most influential voice for morality and peace in the world in the last 100 years." Michael Ireland, "Billy Graham: Pope John Paul II Was Most Influential Voice in 100 Years," CBN.com transcript of CNN's *Larry King Live,* broadcast April 2, 2005.

4   David Scott, "The Pope We Never Knew," *Christianity Today,* April 19, 2005, https://www.christianitytoday.com/ct/2005/may/13.34.html.

5   Peggy Noonan, *John Paul the Great: Remembering a Spiritual Father* (New York: Penguin, 2005), 26.

6   Ibid., 30–31.

7   Ibid., 31.

8   Nicholas D. Kristof and Special to the *New York Times,* "China's Hero of Democracy: Gorbachev," archives 1989, accessed May 14, 2018, https://www.nytimes.com/1989/05/14/world/china-s-hero-of-democracy-gorbachev.html.

9   David Aikman, *Jesus in Beijing: How Christianity Is Transforming China and Changing the Global Balance of Power* (Washington, DC: Regnery, 2003), 171.

10 Tom Phillips, "China on Course to Become 'World's Most Christian Nation' within 15 Years," *London Telegraph,* April 19, 2014, https://www.telegraph.co.uk/news/worldnews/asia/china/10776023/China-on-course-to-become-worlds-most-Christian-nation-within-15-years.html.

11 Eric Metaxas, *Miracles: What They Are, Why They Happen, and How They Can Change Your Life* (New York: Dutton, 2014).

12 Jason Zengerle, "Evangelicals Turn Toward … Orthodoxy: The Conversion of Fr. Wilbur Ellsworth," *Journey to Orthodoxy,* July 11, 2010, http://journeytoorthodoxy.com/2010/07/evangelicals-turn-toward-%E2%80%A6-the-orthodox-church-fr-wilbur-ellsworth.

13   Robert L. Plummer, ed., *Journeys of Faith: Evangelicalism, Eastern Orthodoxy, Catholicism, and Anglicanism* (Grand Rapids: Zondervan, 2012), 208–209.

14   Pew Research Center, "America's Changing Religious Landscape," May 12, 2015, http://www.pewforum.org/2015/05/12/americas-changing-religious-landscape.

15   Thomas Reese, "The Hidden Exodus: Catholics Becoming Protestants," *National Catholic Reporter*, April 18, 2011, https://www.ncronline.org/news/parish/hidden-exodus-catholics-becoming-protestants.

16   Plummer, *Journeys of Faith*, 16.

17   Colleen Carroll, *The New Faithful: Why Young Adults Are Embracing Christian Orthodoxy* (Chicago: Loyola Press, 2002), 44–45.

18   Vineworker, "A Legacy of Faith and Unity in Katowice, Poland; Franklin Graham Will Share the Gospel at Christ the King Cathedral in Katowice," *Crossmap* (Billy Graham Evangelistic Association, 2014), accessed February 21, 2015, https://www.crossmap.com/news/a-legacy-of-faith-and-unity-in-katowice-poland-franklin-graham-will-share-the-gospel-at-christ-the-king-cathedral-in-katowice.html.

19   John 10:9.

IMAGE OF *Eight* THE BRIDE, IMAGE OF GOD

*"Open thy mouth for the dumb in the cause of all such as
are appointed to destruction."*

PROVERBS 31:8 KJV

*"Marvel not at the gold and expense
but at the craftsmanship of the work.
The noble work is bright, but, being nobly bright, the work
Should brighten the minds, allowing them to travel through the lights
To the true light, where Christ is the true door."[1]*

PAUL HALSALL

The debate over abortion had been raging even before I was a high school senior in 1973. In the school cafeteria one day, a fellow student showed me the materials she had gathered for her classroom debate on the topic. I still can visualize the image of tattered unborn children.

By the time the US Supreme Court decriminalized abortion, a handful of states had already liberalized their abortion statutes. But no one expected the total eradication of abortion laws that *Roe v. Wade* and

Doe v. Bolton provided. *Roe* declared abortion a constitutional right, and *Doe* paid lip service to the states' ability to restrict late-term abortions. Essentially, the court legalized abortion in the US for any reason and at any time during pregnancy. America became a darker place on January 22, 1973—the day of *Roe* and *Doe*.

But those decisions motivated people from various Christian denominations, other faiths, and even no faith at all to come together to end this horror. I was one of those people.

After our family settled into our new home, I felt restless. I needed a ministry—a cause to devote myself to. I volunteered at a crisis pregnancy center. And in January of 1979, I saw an announcement on television that would enlarge my faith community and expand my pro-life work. The local pro-life group was sponsoring buses traveling to Washington, DC, for the annual March for Life. I arranged for a sitter to watch Angela and Mike in anticipation of a day filled with grown-up conversation.

Calling the number on the announcement to reserve my bus seat kindled a decades-long friendship with the woman who answered the phone. Anne was a wife, a mother, and a registered nurse. She had been an advocate for life even before *Roe* and *Doe,* and she became my friend and mentor. We walked together that January with many others. Over the years, we protested together, lobbied together, laughed together, and came to love each other like family. Every Halloween when my children were young, we visited her home for trick-or-treat.

And there were other friends who impressed me with their commitment to life.

In the mid 1980s, I met John after he had spent a week in a Pittsburgh jail for blocking the entrance to an abortion clinic. At that time, rescue efforts across the country disrupted the abortion business in an effort to discourage women from aborting their babies. John was a young married man. I recall that he and his wife had a few children at that time. Eventually they would welcome ten babies to their family.

Knowing about his rescue and jail experiences, I asked him to speak to the junior high group at my church's Wednesday evening youth program. When he looked into the room and saw about thirty kids, he nearly had a panic attack. After some deep breaths, he rallied, entered the classroom, and inspired us all. Pittsburgh was notorious for its treatment of pro-life rescuers. I thought it funny that thirty junior high kids terrified John, but he was completely okay with being civilly disobedient in a city known for mistreating protesters. In his talk, John didn't dwell on the unpleasantness of his jail experience. Instead, he told us about a vision he had. Driving down the road one day, he envisioned Christ holding a dead unborn baby and weeping over the child. That experience propelled him into the cause for life.

Within the pro-life effort, I found a second faith community. It did not replace my church, but it did give me a new opportunity to live out my faith and convictions and watch others do the same.

The most significant example of unity between Catholics, Orthodox, and evangelicals in America is the response to the *Roe* and *Doe* decisions. Conservative Christianity—Catholicism instantly and evangelicals and Orthodox Christians a bit later—reached out to unwed mothers and the unborn, establishing crisis pregnancy centers and offering abortion alternatives. These ministries often involve people from different Christian traditions and are separate from established churches.

Pro-life ministries work to save mother and child from devastation and destruction. The effort employs a three-pronged approach—educating the public about life issues (not just concerning abortion but also about infanticide and euthanasia and, on the positive side, adoption), helping parents deal with unexpected pregnancies and children already born, and promoting legislation that upholds the right to life from conception through natural death.

Efforts in the political realm have been only marginally successful in protecting human life. But those efforts have kept the issue in front of the public. In spite of more than a generation of legalized abortion, the issue refuses to go away.

And abortion rates are now lower than they have been since *Roe*. While one study's authors credit new, long-term contraceptives for the drop, they acknowledge that they did not investigate causes of the lower numbers.[2] Two Gallup polls from 2009 and 2012 show that support for abortion had slipped to its lowest point since Gallup began asking the question—pro-choice or pro-life?—in 1995.[3] In 2015, the number of pro-abortion Americans climbed slightly, but abortion rates have continued to fall since they peaked in 1990.[4]

Those who support abortion often accuse pro-lifers of caring only for the unborn, of having no regard for the mother or other family members affected by a crisis pregnancy. The accusation is a hasty conclusion that ignores the deep commitment of pro-life people to meet women's needs as well as those of their children, born and unborn, since the mid 1970s. Those who minister through crisis pregnancy centers know their clients' needs are not limited to housing, maternity clothing, and baby supplies. Surviving children (siblings and those who survive the abortion process) and post-abortive parents are walking wounded—struggling with physical, emotional, and spiritual scars. In response, many pro-life organizations have expanded services, offering post-abortion counseling, mentoring, and testing for sexually transmitted diseases. These ministries reach out to post-abortive fathers who either had no say in a woman's decision to abort or regret their role in urging her to it. Moms and dads also often need to learn how to parent and manage a household. Crisis pregnancy centers have grown to meet the many needs of babies and their family members.

And ministries to single parents are not limited to crisis pregnancy centers. In order to meet the needs of low-income parents, many churches now host daycare centers. Unaffiliated with a particular church, Mom's House began in Johnstown, Pennsylvania, in 1983. This ministry cares for children while their parents attend school or career training. Volunteers mentor single parents, teaching them practical parenting and household management skills. Now these parents can complete their education, find employment, and leave welfare. Mom's House now has seven centers in four states.[5] Such ministries, which can be found throughout the US, care for women and *already born* children.

Success stories of changed lives are plentiful. Pro-life Christians encourage our culture to recognize and uphold the sanctity of human life and the primacy of the family. In the meantime, we maintain our personal Christian doctrines and traditions. In no other area of public discourse have Christians worked together as effectively as they have in the pro-life cause—and sometimes with unforeseen results.

Dr. Bernard Nathanson was a central figure in the effort to decriminalize abortion in the US in the late sixties and early seventies. His transition to the pro-life perspective is particularly profound since he was an atheist. I heard him speak in 1980; his intellect and rhetorical skills vastly impressed me. I was unaware—as perhaps he was then—of the transformation sprouting in his heart. He later described his conversion to Christianity as "an unimaginable sequence [that] has moved in reverse, like water moving uphill."[6] I used to joke that I was our local pro-life chapter's token Baptist—a lone Protestant within a community of Catholic life advocates. Dr. Nathanson was the movement's token atheist. His knowledge and experience regarding obstetrical medicine and abortion procedures were, of course, unparalleled within our ranks, and his atheism demonstrated that our cause was not simply one of religious fervor but one of human rights.

Nathanson became pro-life when a career change removed him from the abortion clinic and landed him in an obstetrical office at the dawn of prenatal ultrasound technology. Seeing the reality of preborn children altered his thinking about their humanity. The basis for his new convictions was science, not a foundational belief in the sacredness of human life made in God's image. His arrival at that conclusion was yet to come.

What was the turning point for him spiritually? Was it Christian pro-lifers' devotion to doctrine? Was it our intellectual grasp of the issue of human life? It was neither. It was the self-sacrifice and devotion to God he saw in the pro-life rescue movement—the same fervor that landed my friend, John, in a Pittsburgh jail. Nathanson was the rueful champion of "safe and legal" abortions. As a novice but secular pro-life observer, he witnessed the Christlike attitude of those in the rescue arm of the pro-life cause.

> I had been aware in the early and mid-eighties that a great many of the Catholics and Protestants in the ranks [of the pro-life effort] had prayed for me, were praying for me, and I was not unmoved as time wore on. But it was not until I saw the spirit put to the test on those bitterly cold demonstration mornings, with pro-choicers hurling the most fulsome epithets at them, the police surrounding them, the media openly unsympathetic to their cause, the federal judiciary fining and jailing them—all through it they sat smiling, quietly praying, confident and righteous of their cause

and ineradicably persuaded of their ultimate triumph—
that I began seriously to question what indescribable
Force generated them to this activity. Why, too, was I
there? What had led me to this time and place? Was
it the same Force that allowed them to sit serene and
unafraid at the epicenter of legal, physical, ethical, and
moral chaos?[7]

This tipping point pushed Nathanson into a full-fledged investiga-
tion of Christianity that resulted in him turning his "life over to Christ."[8]

Around the same time, in 1994 a group of evangelical Protestants and
Catholics formed to encourage accord between their two traditions.
Spearheading the effort were Charles Colson, an evangelical, and
Richard John Neuhaus, a former Lutheran pastor who had become a
Catholic priest. With other Catholics and evangelicals, the two signed
and released a declaration entitled "Evangelicals and Catholics Together:
The Christian Mission in the Third Millennium" (ECT).[9]

A noisy controversy followed. Volleys from mainline, liberal branches
of Protestantism accused the signers, both Catholic and evangelical, of
conspiring to further the political interests of the Christian Right.[10] But
Colson's life proves his goals were apolitical. He had once been a right-
hand man to the most powerful man in the world—the president of the
United States. After spending time in prison for his role in the Watergate
scandal, he lived out his Christian convictions ministering in prisons all
over the world. He knew that to change cultures, one must change hearts,
not just engage in politics.

And there was other opposition to ECT. Evangelicals opposed to the
effort accused the declaration's Protestant signers of embracing biblical

error. In 1995, in reply to the controversy, the ECT group issued the book *Evangelicals and Catholics Together: Toward a Common Mission.* The goals of the book's authors included correcting misconceptions and misguided stereotypes about each other's beliefs and cultivating an environment of mutual respect and enrichment. Written by six authors, three evangelical and three Catholic, the ECT book explained areas of agreement: God as creator, the infallibility of Scripture, Jesus' virgin birth, his sacrificial death, bodily resurrection, and eventual return, and the current ministry of the Holy Spirit. The book also acknowledged significant areas of disagreement regarding such matters as the sacraments (or ordinances)—baptism and communion in particular—and each tradition's perspectives on Mary and the saints.[11]

In his chapter, Neuhaus explained the origins of the Protestant-Catholic separation. After Martin Luther's protest, leaders of the Catholic Church met in the city of Trent, Italy, to develop their response to the Protestant Reformation then expanding quickly. They viewed the Reformation claim of salvation by grace alone as a free pass to sin. The apostle Paul had rejected this perspective when he said, "What shall we say then? Are we to continue in sin so that grace may increase? May it never be! How shall we who died to sin still live in it?"[12]

"Cheap grace" is the name Protestant Dietrich Bonhoeffer would later attach to this idea of grace as a free pass. He wrote:

> Cheap grace means the justification of sin without the justification of the sinner ... .
>
> [In contrast, costly] grace ... is the pearl of great price to buy which the merchant will sell all his goods [in order to obtain it]. It is the kingly rule of Christ, for whose sake a man will pluck out the eye which causes him to stumble, it is the call of Jesus Christ at which the disciple leaves his nets and follows him.[13]

Neuhaus pointed out that the council at Trent had in mind James' admonition that faith without works is dead. Because of the different interpretations various sides adopted, Neuhaus wrote, there was plenty of confusion to go around.

> Did the council fathers at Trent misunderstand what the Reformers meant by *sola fide* [faith alone]? Most scholars ... agree that they did not understand the Reformers, especially Luther and Calvin, adequately. And there is slight disagreement, perhaps no disagreement, that the Reformers, especially Luther, could have expressed themselves more clearly, carefully, and consistently. Then too, keep in mind that, apart from Luther and Calvin, there were many who claimed to be advancing the Reformation under the slogan of *sola fide* and who were advocating precisely what Trent thought the slogan meant [cheap grace] ... . That there were misunderstandings is hardly surprising.[14]

Unfortunately, misunderstandings on this issue still endure today.

In 1998, ECT continued the discussion they began in 1995. The group of Christian scholars, leaders, and theologians issued a document titled "The Gift of Salvation." This significant undertaking acknowledged agreement on the doctrine of *sola Christos* (salvation through faith in Christ alone).[15] In 2008, Pope Benedict agreed: "For this reason Luther's phrase: '*faith alone*' is true, if it is not opposed to faith in charity, in love [if it is not cheap grace]. Faith is looking at Christ, entrusting oneself to Christ, being united to Christ, conformed to Christ, to his life."[16] Many Catholics, including all who signed the ECT declaration, believe in *sola Christos*.

Colson said the way to effective accord is through neither universalism nor judgmentalism. "There is a biblical mandate to be discerning, to flee apostasy and lovingly confront those in our midst who are not professing or living the truth." By "the fruit of their lives" we measure whether professing Christians are living the truth.[17] It's the balance between "Do not judge others so that you will not be judged" and "You will know them by their fruits."[18]

In 1996, Neuhaus and Colson were both present at Bernard Nathanson's baptism and confirmation as he entered the Catholic Church.[19] It is beyond ironic that Nathanson became a Catholic. The proabortion movement blamed Catholicism for "the death of every woman [who had died] from a botched [illegal] abortion" and then lied to inflate the number of those deaths.[20] Nathanson's view of the Catholic Church morphed from that of an expedient whipping boy to a guiding light pointing the "way to redemption and mercy through [God's] grace."[21]

What matters least is which Christian tradition Nathanson chose to live out his newfound faith.

What matters most is that he turned his "life over to Christ."

What matters is that he realized that the "New Testament God was a loving, forgiving, incomparably cossetting figure in whom I would seek, and ultimately find, the forgiveness I have pursued so hopelessly, for so long."[22]

Bernard Nathanson regretted his sins, but as an atheist, he had no place to take them. He had been in the darkest possible place. Then he found grace and forgiveness. He saw the wonderful craftsmanship of the Great Master, stepped into the light, and became part of the window. He became a clean piece of illuminating glass.

One-Celled Soul

A one-celled soul you once were.
One cell,
Became eyes, nose, heart, brain, body.
You came crying, laughing into pain, joy,
Rocky path, smooth road, all life holds.
You came,
You who emerged from me,
To change me,
And shine light.

{Endnotes}

1 Paul Halsall, *Abbot Suger: On What Was Done in His Administration,* the Internet Medieval Sourcebook, trans. David Burr, Fordham University, January 1996, accessed June 27, 2016, https://mediaevalmusings.wordpress.com/2012/10/03/light-upon-light-abbot-suger-and-the-invention-of-gothic.

2 Sandhya Somashekhar, "Study: Abortion at Lowest Point Since 1973," *The Washington Post,* February 2, 2014, https://www.washingtonpost.com/national/health-science/study-abortion-rate-at-lowest-point-since-1973/2014/02/02/8dea007c-8a9b-11e3-833c-33098f9e5267_story.html?noredirect=on&utm_term=.44d8f5314a65.

3 Lydia Saad, "'Pro-Choice' Americans at Record-Low 41%," Gallup, May 23, 2012, http://news.gallup.com/poll/154838/pro-choice-americans-record-low.aspx.

4 Lydia Saad, "Americans Choose 'Pro-Choice' for First Time in Seven Years," Gallup, May 29, 2015, http://news.gallup.com/poll/183434/americans-choose-pro-choice-first-time-seven-years.aspx; National Right to Life Committee, "New Guttmacher Study Shows Abortion Numbers Hit Historic Low," January 17, 2017, https://www.nrlc.org/communications/releases/2017/release011717.

5   Mom's House, accessed July 3, 2014, http://www.momshouse.org.

6   Bernard Nathanson, *The Hand of God: A Journey from Death to Life by the Abortion Doctor Who Changed His Mind* (Washington, DC: Regnery, 2013; first published, 1996), 193.

7   Ibid., 199.

8   Rev. C. John McCloskey III, "Foreword," ibid., xiv.

9   This statement is provided in full in Charles Colson and Richard John Neuhaus, eds., *Evangelicals and Catholics Together: Toward a Common Mission* (Dallas: Word, 1995), xv–xxxiii.

10   Ibid., 178.

11   Ibid., xviii, xix.

12   Romans 6:1–2.

13   Dietrich Bonhoeffer, *The Cost of Discipleship*, trans. R. H. Fuller (New York: Touchstone, 1995; first published, 1959), 44–45, as quoted by Shane Vander Hart, "Dietrich Bonhoeffer: Cheap Grace vs. Costly Grace," *Caffeinated Thoughts*, June 3, 2010, https://caffeinatedthoughts.com/2010/06/dietrich-bonhoeffer-cheap-grace-vs-costly-grace.

14   Richard John Neuhaus, "The Catholic Difference," in Colson and Neuhaus, *Evangelicals and Catholics Together*, 209.

15   Colson, Neuhaus et al, "The Gift of Salvation," *First Things*, January 1998, accessed May 21, 2014, https://www.firstthings.com/article/1998/01/001-the-gift-of-salvation.

16   Pope Benedict XVI, General Audience, Saint Peter's Square, November 19, 2008, http://w2.vatican.va/content/benedict-xvi/en/audiences/2008/documents/hf_ben-xvi_aud_20081119.html.

17   Colson, *The Body*, 89. Colson's endnote to this passage lists Matthew 7:15–23, 12:33–37, and Luke 6:43–45, all NASB.

18   Matthew 7:1, 16.

19   Nathanson, *The Hand of God*, xi.

20   Ibid., 91–92.

21   Ibid., 200.

22   David Kupelian, "Dr Bernard Nathanson: Abortion Activist and Historian," *WorldNetDaily*, as cited by Life.org.nz, 2011, accessed May 15, 2015, http://www.life.org.nz/abortion/aboutabortion/historyglobal9.

Nine
CLEANING THE GLASS

"[A]nd My people who are called by My name will humble themselves and pray and seek My face and turn from their wicked ways, then I will hear from heaven, will forgive their sin and will heal their land."

2 CHRONICLES 7:14

"[D]irt, soot, and grime can build up on both sides of [stained] glass from pollution, smoke, and oxidation. In churches the traditional burning of incense or candles can eventually deposit carbon layers. These deposits can substantially reduce the transmitted light and make an originally bright window muted and lifeless."[1]

NEAL A. VOGEL

Six months after I became a mother, my own mother passed away from congestive heart disease. She was only fifty-four, and I was only nineteen. Her illness took her quickly, and there was no time for the kind of healing conversations that might have reduced my regret after she was gone.

After she died, Dad decided to sell the house and move into a small apartment. As we were helping him prepare for his move, my brother and I were cleaning the attic and musing over some of our finds. I still have two—a silver sugar bowl and a veneered dresser that sits in my dining room. But our most fascinating treasure was inside the top drawer of the otherwise empty dresser—a letter Dad had written to his future mother-in-law, Mother Miller, as he called her.

He was writing from California where he was waiting to deploy to the uncertainty of the South Pacific during World War II. He wrote of his sense of "blank thrill"—a combination of "the feeling of the unknown and also adventure." He discussed how much he enjoyed the navy and how glad he was to be with the men beside him. He expressed his eagerness to return to those he loved after the war. "Back home, I have a wonderful collection of friends; good ones. You and your family come first, Nan of this group being first. She means everything in life for me— and to think about her and the two of us together after the war makes all this worthwhile."

Dad wrote of three things that gave him a sense of security. First was his assurance in the men he was with: "in our commanders and the reason we are going, also we will be successful in our detail." The second was his friends at home and "the strength my love for Nan gives me and hers for me." His third source of strength was his "faith and trust in God." The first two addressed "my worldly cares, the last, my spiritual ... I can leave tomorrow satisfied completely in everything I live for. Not a question in my mind of a thing left undone, or a word unkindly said, not righted, not a care." The letter was dated August 10, 1942, eight months after the Japanese attack on Pearl Harbor.

Years later I mentioned the letter to him. "I was saying goodbye" was his response, "just in case."

The part of the letter that has always stuck with me is that he left "no word unkindly said, not righted." He had done all he could to make everything right with everyone he was leaving behind. He might have been able to convince himself that he didn't have time to fix things with everyone or that whatever he had done wrong was not a big deal. Instead, "just in case," he had made things right.

I spent many years dwelling on the sins of my husband before I fully acknowledged my own. I told myself that his sins were of greater magnitude than mine and the cause for justifiable bitterness. My own sins were tiny, long ago, easily explained away as the result of immaturity and, therefore, easily forgiven. Year by year conviction peeled back layers of self-justification and excuses. I marveled that so many years after the poor decisions I made, the consequences of my sin had such weight.

I can look back now and see that God redeemed and restored much that my sin could have destroyed forever.

Up close and personal, the other person's sins always seem bigger than our own. We don't see the judgmental beam in our own eye for the speck in theirs. Inevitably, hindsight comes closer to 20/20. As the image of the window becomes clearer, so does the reflection of ourselves in it.

Time gives us the objectivity to see two sides where before we could only see one. We realize that we too are not without sin. We have no stones to throw. We can give forgiveness and ask for it too. The perspective of time gives us the opportunity to repent of sins that might seem long ago and far away. Only Christ, through our true repentance, can wash them away.

Repentance is how we start to restore the image of the Bride, not in a public relations sense, but in a biblical one. And repentance begins with the faithful.

Why the faithful? Isn't repentance something for the unbelieving population to grasp—those we perceive are messing up the world and dragging our culture into a downward spiral? Yes, it's something they need to do to become part of the Bride, part of the picture. But the kind of repentance that can turn the world around is for us. It's for his people already in the church.

I didn't come to this idea on my own. I'd been praying for our nation to turn back to God, but in my mind that always involved something someone else needed to do. I'll pray. I'll watch. I'll work when I can. I'll cheer when it happens.

At brunch one day, my longtime friend, Renee, dropped a brick of truth on my head. "He calls *his own* people to repentance—*my* people ... called by *my* Name."

That is me.

That is us.

The first two kings of Israel, Saul and David, are a study of contrasts. Each king had a prophet. Each one sinned. Only David repented.

Saul's prophet was Samuel. Impatient Saul carried out a sacrifice, refusing to wait for Samuel who was supposed to perform it. Afterward, he explained to Samuel that he acted "Because I saw that the people were scattering from me, and that you did not come within the appointed days, and that the Philistines [the enemy] were assembling at Michmash."

Saul listed his motivations; maybe they sounded reasonable to him. Maybe they sounded silly as he listed them aloud for Samuel, who said, "You have acted foolishly; you have not kept the commandment of the LORD your God, which He commanded you, for now the LORD would have established your kingdom over Israel forever."[2] Saul stepped out of his role as king and into the wrong role of priest. But instead of confessing and repenting, he tried to justify himself.

David had a prophet too. When David committed adultery, impregnated the woman, and then arranged to have her husband killed to cover his crime, the prophet Nathan confronted him. Unlike Saul, David did not give a list of excuses. His response was, "I have sinned against the LORD."[3]

Saul and David both offended God. Saul made excuses and wore a false face before the people. David was transparent before God and Nathan. That difference set in motion the events that would remove Saul's line from the throne of Israel and establish David's in the line of Christ.

Many churches have turned the volume way down on the discussion of repentance and are blasting the message of God's love. But we won't find blessing unless we refuse Saul's methods and adopt David's.

Our news sources daily spew stories of atrocities accompanied by many excuses and little repentance. Sometimes we are aghast at what people try to justify: mass shootings, rape, looting, riots, and the list goes on.

There is a sense that my rights are sovereign and yours are nonexistent. Many in the church have bought into that message. Instead of confessing our sins and maintaining transparent lives, we justify our sins, deceiving ourselves that they don't exist or simply don't matter.

We can't expect the world to exhibit behavior we don't model. When we model repentance, others see David instead of Saul. Repentance is the first step on a life journey when we determine to follow Christ, but it's also a frequent stopping place along the way—a place where we check our direction and retool our priorities, letting him reshape our attitudes.

Repentance produces changed people.

Repentance produces anointed, effective ministry.

Rather than being a negative burden, repentance is an overtly *optimistic* act.

God commands us to "confess your sins to one another, and pray for one another *so that you may be healed*."[4] Sin and life's burdens weigh us down. On top of those burdens, we add the pressure to appear perfect. Acknowledging our reality and letting others into that reality is uncomfortable, but that is where healing happens. There is no other way for us to "bear one another's burdens, and *thereby fulfill the law of Christ*."[5] That's important, and we often overlook it. Sharing our burdens with one another fulfills the law—not just our prayer requests for that new job or relief of our child's ear infection—but our *burdens*, what weighs us down and holds us back. Letting each other know our sins is uncomfortable. But confessing our sins to each other brings healing.

Our burden carrying is an area of authentic disagreement between our traditions. Much of that disagreement centers on a dispute about translation, but it also has elements of misunderstanding.

For Catholic, Orthodox, and some reformed Protestant denominations, confession is between a penitent person and a priest. The priest hears the person's sins and may assign penance—something for the confessing person to do. That practice is based on an interpretation of the Greek word for penance that carries with it elements from the Old Testament. The liturgical view from early church scholars weaves continuity between the Old and New Testaments regarding repentance. This perspective carries the idea of sorrow over our sins and making reparations.[6]

The evangelical view rejects the practice of priestly confession. Evangelicals translate repentance in the New Testament with a more positive emphasis. It indicates moving in a new direction, turning away from sin to a new way of life. It is "not a confession of sins but a change of mind."[7]

A voice often overlooked in the dispute is the Greek Orthodox tradition, which has no need to translate from the original Greek. This tradition can't fall victim to mistranslation since it doesn't need to translate. In Orthodoxy, repentance "denotes a change of mind, a reorientation, a fundamental transformation of outlook, of man's vision of the world and of himself, and a new way of loving others and God ... . To confess is not so much to recognize and expose a failure as it is to go forward and upward, to respond from within to the calling of God."[8] That explanation seems to fit the evangelical view of repentance—which would not require a formal confession to a priest. Yet Orthodox practice includes confession and penance.

Critics of liturgical traditions often point to the practice of confession when they say that Catholics and Orthodox believe in salvation by works rather than by faith. The work of confession, these critics assert, is like a ticket to heaven. A confessing sinner may feel free to keep sinning so long as he intends to confess his sins. He would make grace cheap. But in both Catholic and Orthodox practice, confession is the means to repentance. It is a turning away from one's sins, not steeping oneself in them. And it's important to remember that, while Luther affirmed faith rather than works for salvation, he still endorsed the practice of confession with penance and encouraged it. And when Luther translated the Scriptures into German, he maintained the Catholic sense of penance.[9] Luther did not see confession as a work sinners could use to gain heaven. Many Lutherans and other liturgical evangelicals still practice private confession today.[10]

Further, both Catholic and Orthodox traditions assert that it is not priests who actually forgive sins. According to Catholic teaching, "Only God forgives sin."[11] Russian Orthodox practice emphasizes that same doctrine as the priest reminds the person confessing, "I am merely a witness." At this point, the priest may "impose a penance ... but this is not an essential part of the sacrament and is very often omitted."[12] My son's recent penance asked him to "focus on the cross" for a day to help him turn from his sin and come closer to God.

Protestants often misunderstand priestly confession. I know I did even as a Catholic child. I was surprised as an adult to hear some of my Catholic friends laud a particular priest as a "fabulous confessor." Instead of the confessional intimidating them, they had found in this priest a valuable counselor. His knowing their sins was helpful to them in overcoming them.

Likewise in Orthodoxy, the priest "gives advice." Unlike Catholic confession where a screen separates priest and penitent, in Orthodox confession, priest and penitent face each other "in any convenient part of the church."[13] Confession is a time when repentant sinners obey the command to confess their sins and receive discipleship and healing.

In the debate over the necessity of a priest to obtain absolution, many evangelicals have rejected the need to confess altogether. I believe, however, that this is disobedience that robs us of the healing God promises as the result of our confession. The transparency of confession heals us and produces healing in others. Admitting our sins to a trusted confidant helps us put in perspective our struggles to reflect Christ's righteousness. Admitting our sins—at least some of them—publicly, as part of our testimony, enhances our transparency and helps us better disciple others. But any public confession of sin must be met with compassion and humility. Anyone confessing anything must feel safe enough to open up. Safety comes from the compassion and humility of other believers.

However, safe, compassionate, and humble are not always what the penitent receive from public confession in our churches. Author Anne Jackson tells the story of "Missy" whose church singled her out at a special meeting convened so the teen girl could "confess" to the congregation her state of unwed expectancy. "Missy's own Hester Prynne experience taught [Jackson] that personal confession is too big to be entrusted to an entire institution." "Missy was never again just Missy. She became Missy the project, Missy the Girl Who Got Pregnant and Stood Up in Front of the Entire Church." In telling Missy's story, "Jackson's goal is to provoke churches toward creating a culture where members can speak freely about their mess."[14] That is a key component to confession, whether it occurs in a private or public setting. Missy the project would still have been Missy the teenage girl if only her congregation hadn't been pretending that Missy (Gasp!) had been the only one of their flock to sin. She could have kept on being just Missy if she had confessed to a compassionate, transparent congregation of fellow stumblers who would love and accept her.

This difference between our traditions is often a justification we use to avoid working together. On the surface, varying doctrines appear to be the biggest roadblock to accord. Looking beneath the surface, we come up with another answer: Our pride divides us. In order for my way to be right, yours has to be wrong. Self-justification closes doors; admission of our own faults opens them.

Confession, they say, is good for the soul. When we let others see who we truly are, they can be transparent with us. We can become companions who mentor and disciple each other. Mentoring helps us find a new path in life. Discipling includes bearing one another's burdens, and confession is part of that. Discipling helps us navigate our new path in faith that grows as it goes.

Christ is the Great Forgiver and the Great Physician who cleans the glass. The repentant church in accord radiates the image of the window in vivid clarity.

"I wish," Scrooge muttered, putting his hand in his pocket, and looking about him, after drying his eyes with his cuff: "but it's too late now."

"What is the matter?" asked the Spirit.

"Nothing," said Scrooge. "Nothing. There was a boy singing a Christmas Carol at my door last night. I should like to have given him something: that's all."[15]

CHARLES DICKENS

{ENDNOTES}

1   Neal A. Vogel and Rolf Achilles, "The Preservation and Repair of Historic Stained and Leaded Glass," National Park Service, Technical Preservation Services, October 2007, https://www.nps.gov/tps/how-to-preserve/briefs/33-stained-leaded-glass.htm.

2   1 Samuel 13:11–13.

3   2 Samuel 12:13.

4   James 5:16, emphasis added. The rest of the verse says, "The effective prayer of a righteous man can accomplish much." Righteousness follows repentance, not the other way around.

5   Galatians 6:2, emphasis added.

6   Brian Pizzalato, "Old Testament Events Prefigure the Sacrament of Reconciliation," *Catholic News Agency*, accessed May 14, 2018, https://www.catholicnewsagency.com/resources/sacraments/reconciliation/old-testament-events-prefigure-the-sacrament-of-reconciliation.

7   Edward J. Anton, *Repentance: A Cosmic Shift of Mind and Heart* (Waltham, MA: Discipleship Publications International, 2005), 33.

8   Greek Orthodox Archdiocese of America, "Repentance and Confession—Introduction," August 17, 1995, https://www.goarch.org/-/repentance-and-confession-introduction.

9   Ibid.

10 Charles Henrickson, "Frequently Asked Questions about an Infrequently Used Practice (Confession)," March 26, 2009, https://steadfastlutherans.org/2009/03/frequently-asked-questions-about-an-infrequently-used-practice-confession-by-pr-charles-henrickson.

11 *Catechism of the Catholic Church*, 1441.

12 Ware, *The Orthodox Church*, 291–92.

13 Ibid., 288–89.

14 Michelle van Loon, "The Trouble with Confessing in Church," *Christianity Today*, September 29, 2010, https://www.christianitytoday.com/women/2010/september/trouble-with-confessing-in-church.html.

15 Charles Dickens, *A Christmas Carol*, Stave Two (London: Chapman and Hall, 1846), Project Gutenberg, released August 11, 2004, https://www.gutenberg.org/files/46/46-h/46-h.htm.

ten
COMPANIONS OF GLASS IN A COMMUNITY WINDOW

*"So we built the wall and the whole wall was joined together
to half its height, for the people had a mind to work."*

NEHEMIAH 4:6

*"Social psychologists and police officers tend to agree that if a window in a
building is broken and is left unrepaired, all the rest of the windows will
soon be broken. This is as true in nice neighborhoods as in rundown ones.
Window-breaking does not necessarily occur on a large scale because some
areas are inhabited by determined window-breakers whereas others are
populated by window-lovers; rather, one unrepaired broken window is a
signal that no one cares, and so breaking more windows costs nothing."* [1]

GEORGE L. KELLING AND JAMES Q. WILSON

In the center of our city sits a beautiful brownstone church with ornately
carved wooden doors and stained glass windows. Elaborate woodwork
and richly painted panels adorn the sanctuary. It is indeed our city's version of the Sistine Chapel.

Our Lady of Mount Carmel Catholic Church opened in 1905. Its founders' intention was to minister to the local Italian community who had immigrated to Altoona, Pennsylvania, largely because work was available at our bustling rail center.[2] Over the next seventy or so years, the church fell into disrepair. A longtime parishioner told me that demolition had been on the table. Instead, after a trip to the Vatican for inspiration in 1979, a conservation company restored the building and saved a landmark.

Halfway across town from the Mount Carmel Catholic Church is Lena's Café where you can enjoy homemade noodles with delectable meatballs and spread roasted garlic on your bread. Only a few blocks from the church is Pacifico's Bakery where the bread Lena's serves is made and where, on Friday mornings, you can buy fresh pepperoni bread. The aroma is amazing! Across the street from the church sits LaJo's grocery store. There you can buy the ingredients to make your very own authentic Italian feasts. These businesses and others blossomed from the tiny Italian community that settled here. Some still thrive today.

In 1905, many men from the neighborhood worked at the railroad alongside men from Great Britain, Ireland, and Germany.[3] Italian children attended the parish school. The men and children became bilingual, while the women often did not because they had access to everything they could want right in their own neighborhood, making learning English unnecessary. With following generations came assimilation and a slow dissolution of the invisible walls encasing this micro-community.

When World War I began, many of the neighborhood men were drafted. Unlike Great Britain whose military units were segregated according to nationality—Irish, Scottish, New Zealander, Australian, British—the American military formed its units based on geography. Like the British Empire, America also had units comprised only of Irish men, for example, since entire neighborhoods in New York City were

Irish. However, the units from places like Altoona would include a mix of people from various ethnic backgrounds.

We tend to remember discrimination as something African-Americans experienced somewhat exclusively. But the Ku Klux Klan didn't just burn crosses to intimidate African-Americans. Especially between 1915 and into the late 1920s, Jews as well as Irish and Italians who happened to be Catholic were also targets of the KKK.[4]

World War II would begin to change things. During those years, while African-Americans were segregated into their own units and Japanese-Americans were interned, other groups from various religious traditions and ethnicities mingled.

The Italian children who attended Mount Carmel Elementary School and then went on to Catholic high school would meet other Catholic students from other neighborhoods. They would eventually find employment that brought them into contact with others of various backgrounds. These Italian men had not only worked alongside German, British, and Irish men, they had also fought two wars beside them. Their combined effort against common foes, including, for some, those from their own homelands, sealed their sense of community here in America.

A couple of generations had changed, not quite everything in this little neighborhood and our nation, but a great deal indeed. In 1944, Mount Carmel Catholic Church, the church built to minister to an Italian community, received an Irish priest.[5] In 1947, Major League Baseball received Jackie Robinson. Times were changing.

In 1960, America elected a Catholic president. Fears that America would become a satellite office of the Vatican did not materialize. Vatican II followed. It inspired the priest's homily I heard as a child announcing a new day in Christendom—the day when we could pray alongside Protestants. With the English (or local language) Mass, Vatican II modified Eucharistic (Communion) prayers and allowed for changes to the liturgical calendar and music.

Still, much did not change—the sacraments themselves, communion, and baptism, for example. In most of Protestantism, those rites are ordinances. And as is the case with confession, some of our disagreement over communion and baptism is authentic. But some is distortion; some is misunderstanding. Determining which is which can help to repair the broken window of our faith communities.

Catholicism takes a literal view of communion drawing from Christ's statement in Paul's first letter to the Corinthians: "when He had given thanks, He broke [the bread] and said, 'This is My body, which is for you; do this in remembrance of Me.'"[6] That view is the doctrine of transubstantiation—that communion becomes the body, blood, soul, and divinity of Christ—not the presence of His old, crucified body but of his glorified, resurrected body.[7]

Orthodox Christians have a similar perspective, but they don't use the term *transubstantiation*.[8] Even so, Catholics and Orthodox are not the only ones who hold that view. R. C. Sproul, a prominent Presbyterian pastor, explained that "there is major agreement among Roman Catholics, Lutherans, Anglicans, and the Reformed that Christ is truly present in the Lord's Supper."[9]

Some Protestants would use the term *consubstantiation*—the idea that Christ's body and blood coexist with the bread and wine of communion. Other Protestants and evangelicals do not accept trans- or consubstantiation, believing communion is a symbol—a metaphor—of Jesus' sacrifice on the cross.

These varying interpretations represent our authentic disagreement.

Distortion of the liturgical viewpoint comes from Protestant/evangelical corners as well as some secularists. These critics compare Catholic communion practices to pagan rituals. There are accusations that Catholic communion is worshiping a sun god or harkening back to the wine-drinking festivals of Dionysius and the mind-altering rites of the Aztecs.[10] Such critics ignore the shared views of other liturgical denominations, reserving their criticism for Catholicism.

Rather than reflecting pagan practices, the Catholic Church, along with some Protestant denominations, draws a parallel between Communion and the Passover meal Christ was commemorating with his disciples during the Last Supper.[11] The Hebrews in captivity sacrificed a lamb and applied its blood to their doorways to protect them from the judgment coming to the Egyptians. The lamb foreshadowed the Lamb of God—Jesus Christ—his blood applied to believers, then and now.

Christians who distort Catholic teaching about communion feed separation. They walk in league with secularist critics who falsely, if unwittingly, promote distortion. Our Christian disagreement over baptism is less one of distortion and more one of misunderstanding. When we misunderstand each other's practices, we miss a vital piece of perspective.

In Catholicism, baptism marks the church welcoming a child or convert into community.[12] That welcoming illustrates the perspective of the church as a community. In baptism, a Catholic priest or deacon typically pours water over the person's head, but immersion is permissible—"a legacy of Vatican II." Also, "Baptism is the first step in a lifelong journey in commitment and discipleship." Catholics believe baptism washes away sin, including original sin—the sin of Adam and Eve.[13]

Orthodox baptism includes infants as well as older converts and is conducted by immersion. It signifies the person's death to self and rising to new life, as Christ did by dying on the cross and resurrecting. Baptism becomes "the act of a person's death and resurrection in and with Jesus. Christian baptism is man's participation in the event of Easter." Orthodox baptism removes ancestral sin, which differs from original sin. Ancestral sin means we bear the consequences of the first sin—Adam and Eve's disobedience—but not personal guilt for it.[14]

The idea that baptism removes sin is an example of authentic disagreement between liturgical traditions and evangelicals, as is infant baptism.

In some Protestant reformed traditions, baptism represents a covenant, which, like Catholic baptism, includes infants. This view hearkens to biblical passages that report the baptisms of entire families (Acts 16:15, 33), as the view of Catholic baptism also does.[15] And it points to the Old Testament covenant God made with Abraham and symbolized by circumcision.[16] Circumcision represents the Abrahamic covenant in which God promises Abraham that he will "bless those who bless you, and the one who curses you I will curse. And in you all the families of the earth will be blessed."[17] Circumcision is the symbol of the Jews' connection to God. It foreshadowed Christ's coming, which would bless all the families of the earth. From the covenantal and liturgical perspectives, baptism symbolizes the covenant between God, parents, and their child being baptized.

Just as infants were circumcised before they could understand faith, infants in these traditions receive baptism. But every Christian tradition calls the child to a life of faith. Baptism is not a free ticket without subsequent faith.

For many Protestants and evangelicals, baptism involves immersing the person's entire body in a symbolic act that represents a decision to follow Christ. Someone must decide to be baptized—a requirement that excludes infants. This form of baptism represents the beginning of a new life going in a new direction—and it's a new path the believer has willfully determined to walk.

Every Christian tradition, with rare exception,[18] affirms the practice of baptism. And every tradition within Christian orthodoxy performs baptism in the name of the Father and the Son and the Holy Spirit. Our baptism practices reflect our perspectives of the church itself. Liturgical Christians view the church as a community of companions. Evangelicals view the church as companions in community. Christianity works best when companions and community work in support of others.

*"To sit in the theater of God and see His glory crack
the dark, to open the eyes of my heart to see the fountain
of His grace—thousands of gifts—I have to split heart
open to more and more of Jesus."*[19]

ANN VOSKAMP

{ENDNOTES}

1   George L. Kelling and James Q. Wilson, "Broken Windows: The Police and Neighborhood Safety," *The Atlantic,* March 1982, https://www.theatlantic.com/magazine/archive/1982/03/broken-windows/304465.

2   Accessed July 1, 2015, http://mountcarmelaltoona.weebly.com/history.html.

3   "Pennsylvania Railroad Shops Historical Marker," ExplorePAhistory.com, accessed May 16, 2014, http://explorepahistory.com/hmarker.php?markerId=1-A-1D6.

4   George J. Marlin, "The Ku Klux Klan and American Anti-Catholicism," *The Catholic Thing,* November 30, 2011, https://www.thecatholicthing.org/2011/11/30/the-ku-klux-klan-and-american-anti-catholicism.

5   Our Lady of Mount Carmel Parish, Our History, 2006, accessed July 14, 2016, http://mountcarmelaltoona.weebly.com/history.html.

6   1 Corinthians 11:24.

7   The Committee on Doctrine of the United States Conference of Catholic Bishops, "The Real Presence of Jesus Christ in the Sacrament of the Eucharist: Basic Questions and Answers," 2001, accessed July 18, 2016, http://www.usccb.org/prayer-and-worship/the-mass/order-of-mass/liturgy-of-the-eucharist/the-real-presence-of-jesus-christ-in-the-sacrament-of-the-eucharist-basic-questions-and-answers.cfm.

8   Fr. John Breck, "Why Not 'Open Communion'?" Orthodox Church in America, June 1, 2007, https://oca.org/reflections/fr.-john-breck/why-not-open-communion.

9   R. C. Sproul, "The Battle for the Table," Ligonier Ministries, accessed July 15, 2016, https://www.ligonier.org/learn/articles/battle-table.

10 Ocean Malandra, "The Pagan Origin of Communion," People of Our Everyday Life, September 29, 2017, https://classroom.synonym.com/the-pagan-origin-of-the-communion-12087032.html; Timothy M. Youngblood, "Eucharistic Adoration: Sun Worship?" *The Master's Table,* accessed July 15, 2016, http://www.masters-table.org/pagan/sun1.htm.

11 Brant Pitre, "The Jewish Roots of the Mass," Catechetical Sunday, United States Conference of Catholic Bishops, September 18, 2011, http://www.usccb.org/beliefs-and-teachings/how-we-teach/catechesis/catechetical-sunday/eucharist/upload/catsun-2011-doc-pitre-roots.pdf.

12   Catholic Answers, "How to Become a Catholic," accessed July 14, 2016, https://www.catholic.com/tract/how-to-become-a-catholic.

13   Peter Steinfels, "Many Catholics Choose Baptism by Immersion," *New York Times*, March 25, 1989, https://www.nytimes.com/1989/03/25/us/many-catholics-choose-baptism-by-immersion.html; Saint Richard Catholic Church, "Baptism," accessed May 14, 2018, http://saintrichard.com/about/baptism; Peter Nathan, "The Original View of Original Sin," *Vision*, Summer 2003, http://www.vision.org/visionmedia/article.aspx%3Fid%3D227.

14   Orthodox Church in America, "The Sacraments: Baptism," in *The Orthodox Faith*, vol. II (Department of Religious Education, Orthodox Church in America, 1981), accessed July 14, 2016, https://oca.org/orthodoxy/the-orthodox-faith/worship/the-sacraments/baptism; Orthodox Church in America, "Saint Augustine and Original Sin" (1996–2018), accessed July 14, 2016, https://oca.org/questions/teaching/st.-augustine-original-sin.

15   Rev. David Feddes, "Should Babies Be Baptized?" Christian Reformed Church, January 13, 2002, https://www.crcna.org/welcome/beliefs/position-statements/baptism/should-babies-be-baptized; Tim Staples, "Infant Baptism," *Catholic Answers*, October 4, 2014, https://www.catholic.com/magazine/online-edition/infant-baptism.

16   Rev. Michael Glodo, "Covenant Sign and Seal: The Symbolic Significance of Circumcision, and Its Application to the New Testament Believer, Part 1 of 2," *Third Millennium Ministries Magazine Online*, vol. 3, no. 20 (May 14–20, 2001), http://www.thirdmill.org/files/english/html/th/TH.h.Glodo.Signs.1.html.

17   Genesis 12:3.

18   "Why Does the Salvation Army Not Baptize or Hold Communion?" Waterbeach Salvation Army Community Church, accessed July 15, 2016, http://www.waterbeachsalvationarmy.org.uk/what-to-know-more/why-does-the-salvation-army-not-baptise-or-hold-communion.

19   Ann Voskamp, *One Thousand Gifts: A Dare to Live Fully Right Where You Are* (New York: Zondervan, 2010), 116.

Eleven
FRAMEWORK FOR THE IMAGE

_"[Y]ou also, as living stones, are being built up as a
spiritual house for a holy priesthood, to offer up spiritual
sacrifices acceptable to God through Jesus Christ."_

1 Peter 2:5

_"The lead framework for stained glass windows is the chief
support of stained glass. Like the bony skeleton, it is rigid
where essential, yielding where necessary, compliant always."[1]_

Anita and Seymour Isenberg

The Holy Spirit moves each piece of glass to its assigned posts within the framework of the Master's plan. Without the framework, we would be disordered pieces of glass unable to convey the image of the window. As glass pieces take their places, they become the image and show the work of the Master.

In early 1987, after eleven years as a stay-at-home mom, I found part-time work at a local bank. The environment was pleasant, but the transition was huge. My faith community became the support, the framework that helped my family navigate the huge changes we faced.

The support we received helped us move forward when we may have found ourselves stuck.

In order to work, I had to find care for my children. The older ones were in school, so I placed my two youngest children in the care of first one friend and then another. Through an acquaintance at church, I discovered that our community had a federally subsidized daycare center—by far the most affordable option.

By early 1988, I had been on my own with all my children for three years. Now divorce loomed. My marriage had broken three years earlier; now its end would be official. There would be no permanent return to my dream job of full-time cookie baker. I needed a new plan.

My job as a bank teller taught me that I am numerically challenged. Remaining in the banking industry would not be a good career move. I knew that college graduates make more money than high school graduates do, especially graduates like me with little vocational training. At the age of thirty-two, I applied to Penn State and began to consider what I might do when I finished growing up.

An early casualty of my decision to pursue a four-year degree was my children's subsidized daycare. Pursuing a degree disqualified me for care that had been costing me only five dollars a week. The new cost? Forty-eight dollars a week! That was about one-third of my weekly part-time earnings, which would decrease because of my class schedule.

One of my friends from church knew someone who cared for children in her home and was willing to charge me less than the unsubsidized rate. Over the years, several Christian women and teens cared for my children so I could work and go to school. During my last year of school, only my youngest son needed care after his morning kindergarten sessions. We moved on to a new caretaker. The fee she insisted on? Five dollars a week.

God works in ironic ways. Where government regulations threatened to limit my future, God's people stepped in to open my horizons.

I wasn't alone. My small community of Christian women saw my need and stepped out of their personal comfort zones to meet it. They were the framework holding the cracked glass that we were.

The church was once the framework throughout American society. But separation within the church and the pace of modern society have made it more difficult for us to see and meet our neighbors' needs.

When I began to write this book, I assumed President Lyndon Johnson's Great Society was to blame for replacing the church as the benevolent caretaker of our neighbors. What I learned, however, is that government stepped in to fill the void left when many in the church moved away from ministry to avoid the stigma of the social gospel.

After passing tax cuts that President Kennedy had proposed before his assassination, the Johnson Administration received unprecedented tax revenues that increased by 30 percent from $117 billion to $153 billion in just three years. The unemployment rate fell to less than 4 percent.[2] America was awash in prosperity, and the president set about to fix our nation's remaining ills through a set of programs he called the Great Society.

The decades since then have shown that government programs meant to cure our ills have only made them worse. Of course, government intends its policies to help people. Government can help (not necessarily efficiently) someone whose need is purely physical. For example, paid employees can distribute food or the means to procure food. But government cannot fill the need of someone who yearns, not only for food, but also for spiritual affirmation and a sense of transcendent worth. The main function of the church is to be the framework that conveys that affirmation and worth to the shattered.

America moved from the bountiful sixties to the double-digit inflation of the seventies and bounced back to times of plenty in the eighties. For those enjoying prosperity, the notion that someone could easily slip into poverty became less real, more the fodder of fables. We were busy with our own lives. We trusted that government was feeding the poor. We forgot that we are the framework. We are God's plan to help the poor, meeting material needs and affirming worth.

We also forgot that moral fortitude is not something people ingest with their breakfast cereal. In the sixties, milk cartons reminded us to worship during the coming weekend. In the eighties, milk cartons carried the images of missing children. That detail might seem minor, but the shift from the implicit message of "worship is the norm" to "the world is a very frightening place" is huge. Of course, the world has always been a frightening place—more frightening at some points in history than in others. Still, the sixties' milk carton message presents a refuge in a storm; the eighties' message presents only a shipwreck. Something culturally significant had changed—and not for the better.

The shift from American churches meeting the spiritual and physical needs of the poor to the American government meeting only physical needs was seismic, with ramifications that echo into each ensuing generation. Yet government increased spending without ever solving the problem of poverty. Just as social spending increased during the Johnson Administration, it also increased during the Reagan and George H. W. Bush administrations—102 percent from 1980 to 1993. Today, the numbers continue to climb.[3] And something else climbs along with high taxes and government's failure to solve social problems effectively—public resentment. People resent the lack of return on their tax dollars. They expect what they pay in taxes to sufficiently fill needs without extra giving. Why should they give to the poor through their church when they're already paying a high tax bill?

And there is a perception that many who rely on government help follow a family history of dependence. Yet, intergenerational dependence is less entrenched than many of us realize. Research shows that "although welfare does not ensnare the majority of its users, it does encourage dependency by many of the most vulnerable recipients." Those most vulnerable are "unmarried mothers [who] will have the longest durations" of need. The average time on assistance for a single mother is twelve years.[4]

A great abyss lies between dependence and self-reliance. Welfare programs are supposed to provide a safety net to fill needs but build few bridges to self-reliance. It's hard to navigate the abyss without a bridge. That regulations made my childcare costs increase when I was trying to expand my own earning power serves as an example.

The problem involves more than social policy, although social policy is deeply embedded in the problem. The welfare system traps some people, and I understand why it is so difficult for them to get out.

Here's how the system ensnares.

When I began to work at the bank, I started savings accounts for each of my children, mostly with money they received as gifts for birthdays or Christmas. But the welfare system counted that money as *my* assets and reduced the amount of aid we received. Their accounts barely stretched beyond the minimum balance ($100) that would protect their savings from service charges. Eventually, money got so tight that, little by little, even their meager savings disappeared. Ironically, eliminating their savings brought more aid into our home.

By the time my daughter, Angela, got a part-time fast-food job during her high school years, we were no longer receiving food stamps. If we had been, her earnings would have counted toward our household income. Why would a teen get a part-time job for spending money if she knew her mother would lose the family's food assistance? The system effectively discourages savings and entry-level work, bridges that would span the abyss.

Social policy implements an either/or philosophy: either you are in serious need or you are not. Somewhere between serious need and sufficiency is where the church can build the bridge to independence for so many.

That's why it's hard to get out. And here is another way it's hard— and it has little to do with the system.

My earnings as a bank teller were better than minimum wage, but my hours were limited to fewer than twenty per week. My paycheck and child support still did not completely fill our needs at the time, so that's how we ended up applying for food stamps. Applying involved hours of waiting in the welfare office and a lengthy documentation of my situation, followed by monthly trips to a bank to acquire the food stamps.

One month, I went to a local branch office where I had not yet worked to pick up my food stamps. No one who worked there knew me. With me was my son, Chris, probably about six or seven years old at the time. When the teller waiting on us realized why we had come to the bank that day, her demeanor immediately changed. She became cold and rude. I wanted to explain that I too was a bank employee, that I had not chosen my situation.

I looked at my son; he had not seemed to notice her air of resentment. I didn't want him to share the shame I felt by calling his attention to her attitude. I briefly flirted with the idea of sending him to the entrance to wait for me so I could explain that I did not deserve this woman's disdain—that no one did. Instead, I walked away wanting to protect Chris' innocence more than I wanted to justify my worth to this unknowing stranger.

The second instance also involved one of my sons, Rich. When he was seven, he was supposed to bring a snack to school the next day for a class party. Driving him to the store, I decided to allow him a rite of passage he had been begging to experience. Under my watchful eye from the car, he could go into the store, pick out the snack, and pay for it all by himself. I sat in the car and watched through the large plate glass window. He retrieved some cheese curls from the snack aisle and came to the checkout. When he presented his payment in food stamps, I saw that same disdain on the clerk's face that I had seen in the woman at the bank.

It's not hard to see the clerk's perspective. He saw a child buying junk food while he stood for long hours to pay taxes that would fund such purchases. Rich, however, was buying a snack for school, not substituting junk for a meal. But the clerk had no way to know that. I might have wished the teacher had assigned Rich fresh produce instead of a snack, but a bag of chips cost less than vegetables for fifteen children.

Again, I considered going in and saying something to the clerk. Could he justify his resentment? Could he really blame Rich for his dependence? But my son, caught up in the joy of his newfound independence, did not seem to notice. Once more, I chose to remain silent, but the shame burned inside me.

People who knew me had deemed me worthy of help. My community and companions knew our story and wanted to alleviate our need. In the larger society where people did not know how we had come to our state of need, we were pariahs.

I had spent many years believing I indeed had been a victim—a victim of someone else's choice to reject me. I believed my victimhood made me worthy to receive ministry. Eventually, however, I came to realize that I had not been a victim at all. Instead, I had been a prodigal stuck in a cramped pigsty formed of my disobedience. The circumstances of my post-divorce poverty were the consequences of my bad decisions years earlier.

It was my sty, but I was not there alone.

My children had not made any choices that led to our difficult times. The support we received enabled us to crawl through those dark days and off the welfare rolls. Had we remained in poverty, it would only have been a matter of time until my children looked up and noticed someone looking down on them. Perhaps then their view of themselves as pigsty dwellers would become permanent. Had everyone treated us the way the bank teller and store clerk did, we would not have overcome our circumstances.

These events helped me understand how our system of government assistance traps people who might seem unwilling to get themselves out. Those who have never faced poverty tend to think that the poor take the easy way out; they soak the system. Well, some do. For others, perhaps something inside them cracks when they see that look in people's eyes— that look of condescension. Perhaps when people look at them the way the bank teller and the store clerk looked at us, the needy are unable to reject the verdict heaped upon them that they are unworthy.

Today, applying for food assistance is simplified. Recipients are not subject to the disdain of bank employees. But there are still some clerks and store customers who convey resentment through word or manner. A shift away from government dependence would effectively eliminate the resentment some people have toward the recipients of assistance. To someone in need, that resentment can destroy the inner drive to prevail against poverty.

The factors of savings and entry-level work are practical ones. Feeling the resentment of others touches people at their core; it imperils their human dignity.

Government tends to provide assistance *for* the needy; Christian companions can walk *with* them. "Doing *for* rather than doing *with* those in need is the norm. Add to it the combination of patronizing pity and unintended superiority and charity becomes toxic."[5] Christians working in accord can do more *with* those in need and help make poverty a temporary problem instead of a long-term state of being. For the most part, government has failed to understand the distinction between doing *for* and walking *with* the needy. But in a few places, local or state government has grasped the difference between helping and ensnaring. For instance, the city of Pittsburgh is partnering with corporations to fund a mentoring program "to build long term financial stability for urban poor." And former Kansas Governor Sam Brownback established a mentoring program designed to "reduce the amount of time participants rely on" assistance. Brownback's program reaches out to churches to recruit volunteer mentors.[6] Neither effort expects government to effectively help people on its own.

There are other ways Christians can help people cross the abyss. They can periodically "adopt" a child whose parents are absent (literally or figuratively). They can make themselves available after school or on weekends for a neighborhood child or for a community youth program. Many latchkey kids spend hours every week in solitude when a friendly neighbor with milk and cookies could fill the void, help with homework, and encourage them to Christ. Fostering a child from your community, adopting a child domestically or internationally, or simply befriending someone in need are other possibilities.

God dependence coupled with Christian mentoring and discipleship produces social independence and a firmer social structure. Christians can encourage the newly independent to help those who remain in poverty. Mentoring shows people a new path; they, in turn, can show others a new way. Discipleship shows people how to walk their new path in faith. They can show others how to live out faith. Through God's leading, they can become intact pieces of glass in the image of the window.

With a strong framework and intact image, the church can change society. And that change comes about as we encounter broken pieces of glass one at a time.

LOVE FOR THE LEAST

I was unformed in my mother's womb,
When he saw me and formed me for a purpose.
He fed me when I was hungry,
And clothed me when I was naked.
He recognized me when I was the least,
He poured His love on me,
The least of these.

{ENDNOTES}

1   Anita and Seymour Isenberg, *How to Work in Stained Glass* (Radner, PA: Chilton Book Co., 1972), 9.

2   Michael T. Griffith, "The Facts about Tax Cuts, Revenue, and Growth," 6th ed., 2018, accessed June 2, 2018, http://miketgriffith.com/files/taxcutfacts.htm.

3   Daniel Horowitz, "Under GOP in 2017, Government Spending ... Increased $130 Billion," *Conservative Review*, October 10, 2017, https://www.conservativereview.com/news/under-gop-in-2017-government-spending-increased-130-billion.

4   Acton Institute, "Welfare: Separating Fact from the Rhetoric," July 20, 2010, https://acton.org/pub/religion-liberty/volume-5-number-5/welfare-separating-fact-rhetoric.

5   Robert P. Lupton, *Toxic Charity: How Churches and Charities Hurt Those They Help and How to Reverse It* (New York: HarperCollins, 2011), 35.

6   Bob Bauder, "Mentoring Course Opens Doors to 'Urban Poor' in Pittsburgh," *Triblive*, June 14, 2015, http://triblive.com/news/allegheny/8416372-74/mentors-job-course; Bryan Lowry, "Gov. Sam Brownback Announces Mentoring Program for Welfare Recipients," *The Wichita Eagle*. January 7, 2016, http://www.kansas.com/news/politics-government/article53339525.html.

Twelve
MENDING BROKEN PIECES

*"But the vessel that he was making of clay was spoiled
in the hand of the potter; so he remade it into another vessel,
as it pleased the potter to make."*

JEREMIAH 18:4

*"Glass doesn't decompose and is one of few materials
that can be recycled repeatedly."*[1]

SERENA NG

The Master recrafts shattered glass, reshapes it, and gives it new purpose. Glass doesn't lose its value. When we let him, God mends our brokenness and gives us new purpose.

The ministry my children and I received during our time of need came from people who knew of our plight—people from various churches, not just our own, and not just from our tradition. This aid took many forms, including acceptance, encouragement, and guidance, along with occasional material provision. From time to time, we would find boxes of food or clothes on our porch. Sometimes we knew who had brought them; sometimes we didn't. But some people gave more than food. They gave time.

God uses individuals to meet individual needs. Someone took my oldest son, Mike, to get our Christmas tree every December for a few years and installed a basketball rim over our garage. Someone else took Chris to his first Major League Baseball game. Yet another assembled a train set for us one Christmas. That legacy continues as my now adult son, Mike, sets up trains under his Christmas tree every year.

Sometimes God uses communities of people to meet needs. One Thanksgiving, our family received our entire Thanksgiving dinner from an adult Sunday school class.

And sometimes people changed their plans to meet a need. Once, I had a flat tire when I was traveling out of town with one of my children. I had no cell phone, no AAA membership, and a serious fear of strangers. I prayed a ridiculous prayer: "Please, God, send someone *I know* to change this tire." I was an hour away from home; the very idea seemed silly. So I began to teach myself the workings of a car jack. But then I heard someone call my name. A man *I knew* had been traveling a few minutes behind me. Dan drove us to our appointment so that we wouldn't be late, then drove us back to our car and changed the tire.

This story would be amazing enough if it ended here, but it doesn't. Dan also happened to be struggling financially at the time. He needed new tires but didn't have the money to buy them. The next week, someone gave him a new set of tires. A God-wink, indeed.

In spite of all the blessings we received, we still had lean and hard times, but we learned many lessons. We learned how to make do with little. We learned that people, especially Christians who know what you need, are generous and want to help. We saw new ways to fill needs that others—even those who were helping us—did not always realize.

Food and shelter are the most important physical needs, but food stamps don't buy toilet paper, laundry detergent, or shampoo—essential items, to be sure, in a modern society, especially for teenagers. It's easier to tell someone you need food than it is to say you need toilet paper. But people need food. They need hygiene products. They also need encouragement.

When I began college classes, the support of other Christians was invaluable. I was walking where many of them had already gone. They cheered me on, advising me to persevere and offering practical tips for success. A degree would offer me increased employment possibilities—independence that somehow does not seem to come without the encouragement of another.

"Bob" heads up a food ministry in our area. A local church sponsors the ministry, but the volunteers hail from various denominations, Protestant and Catholic. Their work is a picture of accord. One day, a young woman, nineteen years old and with three children, came in asking for food for her family. Her husband, "Frank," had been unable to find full-time employment and had juggled part-time construction work. Bob realized that Frank's lack of a high school diploma was the main reason for his marginal employment. So Bob helped Frank enroll in a GED program. And Frank passed the test. Bob then called the head of the local company where Frank had been working part-time to put in a good word for him. Today, the family no longer needs help from the food pantry. It seems unlikely that Frank was unaware that a GED program was available. He needed encouragement from Bob just as I needed it from those around me.

Working in community provides the opportunity to offer people a broader variety of assistance. For Bob, becoming part of a community effort to feed the needy enabled him to understand, not only this family's urgent need for food but also how to help them toward independence. Community ministry helps us connect people with ways to help themselves. Sometimes, just knowing others' love and acceptance helps people move forward. Bob helped this family move to independence.

Those who give of themselves can help others build independent lives.

❦

In 1986, Laura Schroff befriended Maurice, an eleven-year-old panhandler she met on the streets of Manhattan. His father had been gone for years. His mother was in and out of drug rehabs and fighting a losing battle against addiction. Schroff and Maurice's friendship blossomed as she offered him a weekly meal, first at McDonalds and later in her own home. [2]

The first time they met, she asked him what he wanted to do when he grew up. He didn't know. He had never before known anyone who had a job. Since he had no hopes, he had no dreams. She kept asking. Eventually, possibilities grew in his heart.

One of Maurice's dreams was to have a family who would eat meals together around a large table. That dream sprouted during the first Thanksgiving he shared with Schroff's family. Today, he sits with his wife and children at a large table. They eat together and talk. He had never done that at home as a child.

Because Schroff took the time to get to know and mentor him, Maurice could envision a future different from that of his peers who grew up without such a companion. Maurice's dreams came true because of Schroff's help and because she made herself available on an otherwise busy day. Today, Maurice's children have a different life than the one he had in his youth. Mentors make a difference.

The day Schroff met Maurice, she changed her plans for the day and spent the afternoon engaged in casual conversation. She had no idea whether she would ever see Maurice again. It would have been easy for her to tell herself that giving him her time wouldn't matter—and that the tasks on her schedule really were important. But she didn't. She realized her most important task was sitting right in front of her.

Schroff asked Maurice questions and then listened. Mentors listen and listen well. They walk *with* people. When we take the time to let someone tell us their troubles, we model the patience of God who never seems to tire of listening to endless accounts of our trials. As God meets our needs, we can work to meet others' needs. Schroff met Maurice's needs as best she could, eventually providing clothing for him, an alarm clock so he could get to school on time, and a sack lunch every day that he picked up on his way to school from her doorman.

Mentors listen and then they share. They are transparent about their own failings and situations. Laura Schroff had grown up in a home where alcoholism tormented her father who, in turn, tormented his family. As a young adult, she had been a shattered bride. And her mother died at age forty-seven when Schroff was only twenty-five. As a child, she had struggled in school. When Schroff told Maurice about her own academic challenges, he realized that he wasn't doomed to a life of poverty simply because he found school difficult. Just as she worked hard to make a life for herself, he could too. Showing him a new way to live that he couldn't have imagined before helped him so much, not because her life had been so perfect, but because it had not been perfect. Because she had risen above the imperfections of her life, he could too.

Mentors listen, share, and challenge people. They challenge people to do more than they believe they can. Schroff showed Maurice a new way of living he had only seen on television, a way of life that was mere fantasy to him before he knew her. She brought him close to that kind of life so he could live out his dreams. Life would offer these possibilities to him only if he would make the wise choices that would lead him to them. Schroff challenged Maurice to work for his new dreams. She didn't just give Maurice money and then walk away forever. She gave herself to him. She paid that cost.

What she got in return was the love of a "son" she never had and the devotion of his family to this day.

Laura Schroff picked up the pieces of her own broken life. Then she showed Maurice how to pick up his broken pieces and build a life of his own. There are more Maurices out there in our large and small communities. They wander in darkness. They need the image of the glass to show them how to dream.

Broken Bread

We grow from broken toys to broken hearts.
Broken is usually not a happy word.
It means damaged, inadequate, alone.
But broken bread fixes cracked hearts.
It feeds and fills.
Broken bread restores.

{Endnotes}

1   Serena Ng, "High Costs Put Cracks in Glass Recycling Programs," *Wall Street Journal,* April 22, 2015, https://www.wsj.com/articles/high-costs-put-cracks-in-glass-recycling-programs-1429695003.

2   Laura Schroff and Alex Tresniowski, *An Invisible Thread: The True Story of an 11-Year-Old Panhandler, a Busy Sales Executive, and an Unlikely Meeting with Destiny* (New York: Howard Books, 2011).

Thirteen
SEARCHING FOR BROKEN PIECES

"What man among you, if he has a hundred sheep and has lost one of them, does not leave the ninety-nine in the open pasture and go after the one which is lost until he finds it?"

LUKE 15:4

"You were a jumble of broken bits of glass the sun caught and stained my soul with your colors."[1]

JOHN GEDDES

It was a raw, gray day, and I was glad to be in my warm car when I saw her sitting there with her "Homeless" sign on the cold cement sidewalk. I guessed her age to be between eighteen and twenty. I pulled off the busy street and honked but didn't get out of the car. As I saw her sitting there that day, I did what I often do when I see someone asking for help. I got a gift card out of my purse, put my purse on the floor of the back seat, and wound the window down a few inches.

Prompted by my honk, she came over to the car, her face reflected fear and the icy chill of the day. I don't remember what I said to her. I don't remember what was on my to-do list that day. I do remember her sincere "Thank you" as I handed her the gift card. Then, I drove away. I left her behind, but part of her followed me.

Her fear-filled face still haunts me. What was her story? Why was she there, cold and alone? Why did I not get out and ask her how she ended up in this state? The most obvious and most pertinent question—what else could I have done?—remains unanswered. I had fed my neighbor for part of a day and perhaps encouraged her a bit. But I suspect that my tiny ray of sunshine barely peeked past the mountain of despair she was trying to climb—alone. I have not seen her again.

When a rich young ruler approached Jesus to ask how he could inherit eternal life, Jesus answered in a very interesting way. He listed the man-directed commandments—those concerning our relationships with other people: "Do not murder, do not commit adultery, do not steal, do not bear false witness, do not defraud, honor your father and mother." *So far so good*, the young man thought, since he had "kept all these things from my youth up." But Jesus wasn't finished. Jesus told him to sell all of his belongings and give the money to the poor. The young man could not stand to do that and walked away sad.

That brief summary leaves out some very important details. One is that "Jesus felt a love for him." Jesus spoke out of compassion for *this* wealthy man, not just for the poor who would benefit from receiving the funds from this man's sold possessions. Another detail is that Jesus told the young man to "follow Me." For this man, selling his belongings and following Jesus went together.

Jesus listed the commandments guiding our human relationships, and the man thought he had lived up to them. But Jesus did not directly mention the commandments regarding our relationship with God—having no other gods, rejecting idol worship, guarding God's name, and honoring his day—essentially, loving God most of all.[2] The young ruler did not seem to notice their exclusion. The whole law, the commandments that govern our relationships with both God and other people, is comprised in two words—"Follow Me." For the rich young ruler, his god was his own comfort; he was his own god. He was sad that he couldn't have it all—Jesus *and* the stuff that made him comfortable.[3]

The rich ruler stands in contrast to a lawyer who asked Jesus which commandment is the greatest. Jesus told him that "the whole law and the prophets" are summed up in loving God with all his heart, all his soul, and all his mind, and loving his neighbor as himself.[4] But the man wanted to squirm out of the requirement to love others by narrowly defining his neighbor. He wanted permission to neglect those he found unworthy. He hoped Jesus would agree. But Jesus showed this man his own face in a mirror by telling him the parable of the Good Samaritan. While the religious faithful of the day walked past a crime victim, not wanting to get involved, a Samaritan—a member of the rejected group of the day— stepped up to save the one in need. He was the one who "showed mercy." Jesus told the lawyer to "Go and do the same."[5]

Like the lawyer, we also claim a pass from helping those lying right in our path. We can even point to the teachings of Jesus to try to obtain this pass.

Five chapters after the parable of the Good Samaritan, we find the parable of the Prodigal Son, a story about a father and two sons, one older and compliant, the other younger, rebellious, and foolish. The younger brother insulted the father by demanding his inheritance early and ran off to waste it on sin. He was the "bad" son. The older brother stayed behind, lived obediently, and waited patiently for his inheritance. He was the "good" son.

When the younger son had wasted all his money and became hungry, he decided to swallow his pride, go home, and beg for mercy. A minor role as a servant would be fine, much more comfortable than the pigsty he'd been occupying recently. Certainly, the younger son's deprivation prompted his trip home. Many stop here in the story and declare themselves justified in walking past those who've earned the uncomfortable beds of their own making. If we help them, we only enable them in their sin. It's best—for them—if we just keep walking by. That's what many of us have been telling ourselves.

The story of the Prodigal Son is the third of a set of parables Jesus directed at the Pharisees and scribes. The first is the story of a shepherd who lost one of his sheep. He left the ninety-nine compliant sheep to search for the wayward one, found the wanderer, and placed the sheep on his shoulders for the journey home. He invited his neighbors to celebrate the victory with him. Jesus told his audience of critics, "There will be more joy in heaven over one sinner who repents than over ninety-nine righteous persons who need no repentance."[6]

The second parable tells the story of a woman who lost a precious coin. She searched diligently until she found it and then invited her neighbors to share her joy. Jesus then reiterated that heaven rejoices when a sinner repents.[7]

The third parable breaks the pattern. The father and the older brother "lost" the younger son. No one searched for him. Unlike the major players in the first two parables, the older brother did not desperately search for his sibling and seemed to suffer no torment at all over his loss. Life went on as usual. The older brother continued to work for his father, investing himself in his own inheritance—the reward he was earning through his loyalty and hard work.

The father waited for his younger son to return and watched for him. Even while the younger brother was still a long way off, his father saw him, felt compassion for him, ran to him, hugged him, and kissed him.[8] Representing God, the father's role was to wait, welcome, and celebrate. The older brother is the parallel character to the shepherd and the woman of the first two parables. He was *supposed* to search for his brother.

Upon the younger brother's return and the father's joyful reception of him, the older brother stomped his foot and protested the celebration as an unjust misuse of what should be his own—his inheritance—his just desserts as the dutiful, obedient, "good" son.

Unlike the way Jesus ended the first two stories, he did not provide an application about heaven rejoicing over the repentance of a sinner. Jesus left this story unfinished, with the older brother refusing to celebrate the repentance of the undeserving, "bad" son.[9]

The older brother wouldn't trouble himself to look for his brother, who was unworthy of the grace the father would extend. The father expressed the symbolic joy of heaven when a sinner repents. But having earned his way, the older brother wouldn't share the joy of his father.

In the first two parables, the shepherd sacrificed his time and effort to search for the lost sheep, and the woman worked diligently to find the lost coin. Neither the sheep nor the coin had everlasting value. The older brother was unwilling to sacrifice time and effort to seek his younger brother, an everlasting soul. He did not love the father or the younger brother. He loved only himself.[10]

I did not get out of my car that cold, windy day to find out whether that young woman was a prodigal reeling in the results of her own bad decisions or a wounded traveler aching from the echoes of bad decisions others had made. How she got there, I don't know. How I might have made a difference for her, I still don't know.

I do know who I was that day. I was the older brother—too busy, too afraid, too selfish to befriend someone in need.

But on another occasion, I did get out of the car. I had learned that a woman was standing beside a busy road holding a sign indicating that she needed help. I packed a zip lock bag with some gift cards, snacks, and toiletries and found her. When I arrived, she told me she wasn't homeless. Her husband had just had surgery and "we're just struggling," she said. She hadn't planned a career of standing by the roadway and asking strangers for help. Temporary circumstances had overwhelmed her. She had a problem to solve, but not a problem lifestyle.

It's possible that she deceived me. That she truly was not in need. That's why I try to use gift cards. Gift cards are gifts without strings, and they minimize the possibility of abuse. Most fast-food cards are really only good for food.

Do I ever just keep on walking? Yes.

On a mission trip in Asia, we saw many people begging. One man, quite healthy looking and asking for money, was holding a starving child. The vision of the child's empty, bloated belly cried out to passersby. But as I neared them, a question popped into my head: Why does the man look so healthy and the child so hungry? Because of the language barrier, I couldn't ask the man my question. I continued on my way.

Even in Jesus' intimate group of twelve, one was a deceiver and betrayer. We can't identify all the deceivers. We can, though, seek out broken pieces of glass and let God lead us in our dealings.

Only Christ can meet the spiritual needs of human beings. But his individual followers are the instruments he uses to meet such needs. The church acting in accord is his unified instrument to present himself to the world.

We will not make a difference for every needy person we encounter. Some will refuse the help we offer. Some will turn away from the light. But a few will turn toward it. Some prodigals will come home and let God place them in the image of the window. Then God's light can shine through them into their corner of the darkness.

There are no ordinary people. You have never talked to a mere mortal. Nations, cultures, arts, civilization—these are mortal, and their life is to ours as the life of a gnat. But it is immortals whom we joke with, work with, marry, snub, and exploit—immortal horrors or everlasting splendors.[11]

C. S. LEWIS

{ENDNOTES}

1   John Geddes, *A Familiar Rain* (Buffalo: Chinnok, 2011), n.p.

2   Exodus 20:1–17.

3   Mark 10:17–22.

4   Matthew 22:37–40.

5   Luke 10:37.

6   Luke 15:7.

7   Luke 15:8–10.

8   Luke 15:20.

9   Timothy Keller, *The Prodigal God: Recovering the Heart of the Christian Faith* (New York: Riverhead, 2008), 32.

10   Ibid., 95.

11   C. S. Lewis, *The Weight of Glory* (Grand Rapids: William B. Eerdmans, 1949), 15.

Fourteen
TRUE IMAGE, FORSAKEN VOWS

"I am my beloved's and my beloved is mine,
He who pastures his flock among the lilies."

SONG OF SOLOMON 6:3

"Husband and wife did not need to speak words to one another,
not just from the old habit of living together but because in that one
long-ago instant ... they had touched and become as God when they
voluntarily and in advance forgave one another for all that each
knew the other could never be."[1]

WILLIAM FAULKNER

A few years ago, I attended a Russian Baptist wedding. The bride had been a student of mine, one I had mentored in a small group. A remarkable student with a deep and intelligent faith, she worked hard and read voraciously.

She made a big impression on me one day during her sophomore year when our group was having lunch. She asked that we pray for her friend's mother. The woman had been helping with our school lunch that day but had become ill. After prayer, my student asked permission to go outside to sit with the sick woman who was waiting for her husband to pick her up.

Sometimes the student disciples the teacher.

During another of our gatherings when she was a senior, she told me about her fiancé. "He's already talked with my father," she glowed. She continued in animated excitement. Her father had told the young man that they would have to wait two years before marrying. Young men in this small community usually do not wait two years for a bride, but this young man would.

At the end of two years, the bride's father, a pastor, conducted the ceremony. The service was in Russian, but the church provided electronic translators for the English speakers among us. What unfolded was a beautiful ceremony much like other weddings—until after the bride and groom said their vows. At that point, they both got down on their knees and prayed aloud. Each asked God to "help me keep the vow I just made"—an extra step to reinforce the seriousness of the day.

A fellow teacher and I were among a group of individuals who would speak on behalf of the bride at the reception—another departure from typical weddings. After an amazing meal, I followed along in the program as several others took their turns speaking to the bride and groom. Much of that was in Russian (no translators here). Aunts, uncles, and grandparents, one by one, came forward to give the bride and groom words of wisdom for their life together.

Then came my turn to speak. When I began, the bride stood up. I talked about how impressed I had been with the character of this young woman and related the story of her care for the sick woman in our school cafeteria. I mentioned the radiance I saw in her eyes when she was with her fiancé. When I mentioned the groom, he stood up.

The couple had been up and down throughout the reception. At no point did either of them heave a sigh or roll their eyes. The seriousness they exhibited at the church carried over to the celebration afterward. They would carry it into their lives where they now parent two children.

As we left the reception, I thought of how this joining of two lives had differed from so many others I had witnessed. The mood was just as celebratory—just as joyful. The couple listened respectfully to every speaker. That looked like work to me, and I thought that, at the end of the day, they must have been very tired.

Considering the factors that contribute to divorce, this couple seemed to be at risk. They were young. He did not plan to go to college. She was taking online classes mainly because she wanted to homeschool her children capably, not to enhance her earning capability or empower herself. But consider what they have going for them. They had waited two years as she studied, and he honed and applied his skills as an electrician, increasing his value in the workplace. In the interim, their relationship with each other and extended family continued to develop. Surrounded by family who cared enough to encourage them, whose approval they sought, and whose guidelines they followed, they were part of a close-knit community who witnessed their vows. And they have deep and abiding faith in God.

The more we live out our commitment to Christ, the more stable our families are. The less our society follows him, the less stable our lives are. And in America today, family stability continues to unwind.

God's original plan for the family was stability in traditional marriage. Adam was in the garden, and God said, "It is not good for the man to be alone, so I will create a companion for him, a perfectly suited partner."[2] And God made woman.

Christian marriage is a reflection of the image of the window. The husband represents Christ; the wife represents Christ's bride—the church. Within Christian orthodoxy, marriage is the union of one man and one woman. All of Christian orthodoxy affirms that God intends the husband and wife to remain faithful to each other for life.

Modern society has been bashing these ideas for several decades now. But most people aspire to be married.[3] And it's reasonable to assume that they hope, at least at the onset, that their marriages will last a lifetime.

To some, however, marriage seems outdated. But we forget that in the first century, the idea of Christian marriage was revolutionary. Changing the nature of marriage was a big part of how Christianity turned the Roman world upside down. "In pagan times, a family was a man—the *paterfamilias*, or father of the family—and his property." The mere existence of everyone else in the family depended on the whim of the father. He ruled his personal realm. Wife and children were there for his benefit. If they were not a benefit, they were not there. Abortion was common. And female infanticide was pervasive, claiming the lives of "most" girls. Adultery, especially on the part of men, was customary and assumed.[4]

In contrast, God had established marriage and declared that the man and the woman "shall become one flesh." In the New Testament, Jesus reiterated that "the two shall become one flesh." Christian marriage presented everyone in the family as a sacred, immortal soul. It wasn't just the father who mattered. The wife mattered. The children mattered. Baby girls mattered. To pagan Romans, such thoughts seemed crazy.

Just as crazy was the idea that marriage would be more than an economic arrangement for the man, who in Roman culture was free to engage in sex with anyone (of any age and either gender) at any time.[5] The Christian view of marriage was an exclusive one for both parties. Saint Pope John Paul II explained that marriage is a gift from the Holy Spirit that helps a couple "progress towards an ever richer union with each other on all levels ... [T]he plan of God which was revealed from the beginning ... [supports] the equal personal dignity of men and women who in matrimony give themselves with a love that is total and therefore unique and exclusive."[6] Equal personal dignity. Unique and exclusive. These ideas had never been considered before outside of Judaism. Today all of Christian orthodoxy views marriage this way. Christian marriage is designed to help both parties in the marriage, and by extension, the children. The Orthodox view states: "Becoming 'one flesh' in a blessed marriage is an act of ... selfless giving of one to the other; a self-emptying ... in a manner like Christ when He took on human flesh and assumed human nature."[7]

Liturgical traditions see matrimony as a sacrament. In evangelical churches, it's a rite. Yet there is little dispute about what happens at a wedding. One man and one woman join their lives as a picture of Christ and the church, his bride. Their unity is enhanced by their difference—not by their similarity. People gather to witness them join their lives and ask God to bless that life lived together until the death of one of them. But that isn't how a large percentage of American marriages play out today.

Where have we gone wrong?

The sexual revolution of the 1960s helped spawn radical feminism in the 1970s. We do not have the advantage of hindsight today regarding same-sex marriage, but we can clearly see the results of moral confusion over marriage that reared its head in the 1970s.

Instead of a liberating cure-all the feminists of that day presented, divorce has wreaked havoc on our society. Throughout the decade of the 1970s, no-fault divorce laws swept across most of the country. In their aftermath, divorce rates nearly doubled. Some states have considered tightening their divorce laws, and in New York, the National Organization for

Women effectively protested an attempt to liberalize New York's divorce laws in 2006.[8] Yes, NOW—which had led the vanguard in promoting lenient divorce legislation and unrestricted abortion for decades—was protesting the liberalization of New York's divorce statute. At that time, New York was the lone holdout on no-fault divorce. The proposed divorce bill provided a unique opportunity for NOW to partner with the Catholic Church against allowing one spouse to dissolve a marriage unilaterally. Unfortunately, in 2010, New York finally became the fiftieth state to enact a no-fault divorce law.[9]

We don't have to think hard to understand why the Catholic Church opposed no-fault divorce. But for liberal feminists to turn on a foundational plank of their platform is astonishing. Betty Friedan, author of *The Feminine Mystique*, a catalyst for the women's movement, had called marriage a "comfortable concentration camp." She cheered the passage of the first no-fault law in California in 1970. Twenty-seven years later, Friedan—and NOW—realized that the new laws had harmed women instead of helping them.

Often, men can use custody of the children as a weapon against women. In a perverse game of mental manipulation, the man will agree to forgo a custody battle if the woman agrees to a smaller financial settlement, leaving the woman torn between seeing her children or supporting her children.

One study found that only 37 percent of women retained ownership of the family home under no-fault divorce, versus 82 percent under fault divorce. Another study, conducted by Betsey Stevenson of the Wharton School of Business, found that in states that allow unilateral no-fault divorce, spouses tend to show a lower level of willingness to make financial sacrifices that invest in the future of the other spouse, such as helping to put that spouse through school for a higher degree.[10]

Under no-fault divorce laws, women tend to come up short in battles over finances and property, and they are more likely to lose their health insurance coverage. Today, divorce places 22 percent of divorced women in poverty as opposed to 11 percent of divorced men.

Friedan now admits that feminists "made a mistake with no-fault divorce."[11]

Liberalized divorce laws are a factor in divorce rates, but not the only one. It matters whether the bride and groom are themselves children of divorce. "The risk is 50 percent higher when one spouse comes from a divorced home and 200 percent higher when both of them do."[12] The greater number of divorced parents today means a greater number of divorced adults tomorrow—and the cycle rolls along.

Success in marriage closely relates to economic stability, and economic stability closely relates to success in marriage. It's what W. Bradford Wilcox calls an "increasingly 'separate and unequal' character of marriage" in our nation. Wilcox, a sociologist at the University of Virginia, proposes three strategies churches can employ in response to "the growing class divide in American family life."[13]

The first approach is to lobby for changes to social policies that discourage marriage—increasing child and tax credits for families and eliminating marriage penalties. For several years, I received a tax credit because my income was so low and I was a single parent. I benefitted from receiving tax dollars while I was striving to earn more and become a taxpayer. This benefit helped me tackle some debts that had built up over the year, such as medical expenses. As I earned more, the benefit would gradually decline and allow me to less painfully transition from the status of a tax receiver to that of taxpayer. This tax structure encourages people to earn more, not less. It is a piece of a bridge to help people cross the abyss toward independence.

Wilcox's second recommendation calls for more teaching from the pulpit and more support, perhaps in the form of mentoring, for couples in crisis. So many people today lack the basic skills needed to run a household and sustain relationships. Most millennials don't know how to cook a simple meal, check the pressure in their tires, sew a button on, or perform minor home repairs. That kind of skill can help people gain confidence in maneuvering daily life.[14] Laura Schroff teaching Maurice how to set a table and bake a cake provided him with basic skills he could build on.

The third step Wilcox proposed is the development of ministries for men, especially for the unemployed and underemployed.[15] Women will often gravitate to friendships that provide encouragement. Men in crisis often find themselves in solitude and feeling that asking for help is unmanly. Mentoring ministries for men can provide encouragement and even partnerships with local business and industry to provide training and networking.

But the most important factor in keeping marriages together is faith. Statistics about the success and failure of Christian marriages can be deceptive. The popular perception says that Christians and non-Christians divorce at about the same rate, but that perception fails to consider how invested people are in their faith. A deep faith protects against divorce; a shallow faith actually indicates a greater vulnerability to divorce. One study shows that the rate of divorce for nominal Protestants is 20 percent higher than the rate for secular Americans. But compared to those with no religious affiliation, active conservative Protestants are 35 percent less likely to divorce.[16] Catholics have the lowest divorce rate among other religious affiliations.[17] And one study shows a correlation (a connection but not necessarily a direct cause) between Catholics who use natural family planning and a divorce rate of only 5 percent.[18]

Evangelical Protestants must admit that Catholic doctrine regarding marriage and divorce has been more successful than the more relaxed view often held in Protestant circles.

Faith—the degree of our faith—matters. A lightly applied faith takes God so lightly that we do not value the promises we make to him. A seriously applied faith believes in a serious God and helps us keep the vows we have made.

But family instability doesn't happen just because of divorce. More couples have decided to forego getting married altogether.[19] Instead they live together without any vows at all.

A big problem with cohabitation is its lack of intention. During my Russian student's courtship, everyone involved acted intentionally. The young man asked her father for his daughter's hand in marriage. The two waited and planned. At no time did they act hastily or make a decision based on economics or convenience. Many couples who live together without vows engage in "'sliding, not deciding.' Moving from dating to sleeping over to sleeping over a lot to cohabitation can be a gradual slope, one not marked by rings or ceremonies or sometimes even a conversation."[20] The missing factor is intention.

This "sliding" is a far cry from fairy tale romances in which both parties overcome terrible obstacles finally to emerge victorious and together at the altar. The prince and princess live happily ever after only in the tales because, in real life, obstacles don't vanish at the altar. But with intention, the inconveniences and troubles that do come later make 'the ever' after more bearable at times and more joyful at others. Acting with intention is a cement that keeps married people together. Sliding into marriage only makes sliding out of it easier.

We have encouraged young people to postpone marriage. The typical bride and groom are older today, but the divorce rate has not decreased. The rate of cohabitation has increased. Premarital sex is not a new concept, but as the age of marriage goes up, the likelihood of marriage after multiple sex partners increases. Today, men between twenty-five and forty-four years of age average 6.1 sexual partners before marriage. For women the same ages, the average number of partners before marriage is 4.2.[21]

Those relationships have consequences. Broken relationships cause wounds that accumulate. Scar grows upon scar. The sacredness and lifelong exclusivity of traditional marriage is forsaken. And the number of cracks in the glass keeps growing.

"So the LORD God caused a deep sleep to fall upon the man, and he slept; then He took one of his ribs and closed up the flesh at that place. The LORD God fashioned into a woman the rib which He had taken from the man, and brought her to the man. The man said,

'This is now bone of my bones,
And flesh of my flesh;
She shall be called Woman,
Because she was taken out of Man.'

For this reason a man shall leave his father and his mother, and be joined to his wife; and they shall become one flesh."

GENESIS 2:21–24

{Endnotes}

1 William Faulkner, "The Fire and the Hearth," *Go Down, Moses* (New York: Vintage, 1942, 1994), 104.

2 Genesis 2:18, The Voice.

3 Frank Newport and Joy Wilke, "Most in U.S. Want Marriage, but Its Importance Has Dropped," Gallup, August 2, 2013, http://news.gallup.com/poll/163802/marriage-importance-dropped.aspx.

4 Mike Aquilina and James L. Papandrea, *Seven Revolutions: How Christianity Changed the World and Can Change It Again* (New York: Image, 2015), 55, 60, 61.

5 Ibid., 61.

6 Saint Pope John Paul II, "The Indivisible Unity of Conjugal Communion," excerpted from *Familiaris Consortio*, 1981, accessed August 2, 2016, http://www.fathersforgood.org/ffg/en/month/archive/dec08/unity.html.

7 Fr. George Morelli, "Good Marriage XIII: The Theology of Sexuality and Marriage," Antiochian Christian Orthodox Archdiocese of North America, 2014, accessed August 2, 2016, http://ww1.antiochian.org/node/17964.

8 Robin Fretwell Wilson, "Don't Let Divorce Off the Hook," *New York Times*, October 1, 2006, https://www.nytimes.com/2006/10/01/opinion/dont-let-divorce-off-the-hook.html.

9 *New York Times* editors, "Is New York Ready for No-Fault Divorce?," June 15, 2010, https://roomfordebate.blogs.nytimes.com/2010/06/15/is-new-york-ready-for-no-fault-divorce.

10 Ashley McGuire, "The Feminist, Pro-Father, and Pro-Child Case against No-Fault Divorce," *Public Discourse*, May 7, 2013, http://www.thepublicdiscourse.com/2013/05/10031.

11 Ibid.

12 Nicholas Wolfinger, *Understanding the Divorce Cycle: The Children of Divorce in Their Own Marriages*, as cited by Stephanie Chen, "Children of Divorce Vow to Break Cycle, Create Enduring Marriages," CNN, September 22, 2010, http://www.cnn.com/2010/LIVING/09/22/divorced.parents.children.marriage/index.html.

13   W. Bradford Wilcox, "The Evolution of Divorce," *National Affairs*, no. 35 (Spring 2018), https://nationalaffairs.com/publications/detail/the-evolution-of-divorce.

14   Neil Howe, "Millennials Struggle to Pass Life Skills 101," *Forbes*, July 2, 2014, https://www.forbes.com/sites/neilhowe/2014/07/02/millennials-struggle-to-pass-life-skills-101/#44c5d7b479e7.

15   Wilcox, "The Evolution of Divorce."

16   Glenn T. Stanton, "The Christian Divorce Rate Myth," Ministers Matter, February 14, 2011, http://barryboucher.typepad.com/ministers_matter/2011/02/the-christian-divorce-rate-myth-glenn-t-stanton.html.

17   Adelaide Mena, "Catholics Continue to Have Lowest Divorce Rates," *National Catholic Register*, October 2, 2013, http://www.ncregister.com/daily-news/catholics-continue-to-have-lowest-divorce-rates.

18   Linda Kawentel, "NFP and Divorce Rates: More Research Needed," *The Catholic Conversation*, University of Notre Dame, August 29, 2012, http://sites.nd.edu/thecc/2012/08/29/nfp-and-divorce-rates-more-research-needed.

19   Hope Yen, "Census: Divorces Decline But 7 Year Itch Persists," *The Durango Herald*, May 17, 2011.

20   Meg Jay, "The Downside of Cohabiting Before Marriage," *New York Times*, April 14, 2012, https://www.nytimes.com/2012/04/15/opinion/sunday/the-downside-of-cohabiting-before-marriage.html.

21   Centers for Disease Control, "Key Statistics from the National Survey of Family Growth," June 22, 2017, https://www.cdc.gov/nchs/nsfg/key_statistics/n.htm#numberlifetime.

Fifteen
DARKENING CULTURE,
BRIGHTER LIGHT

*"For God, who said, 'Light shall shine out of darkness,'
is the One who has shone in our hearts to give the Light of
the knowledge of the glory of God in the face of Christ."*

2 CORINTHIANS 4:6

*"Be encouraged that as the world grows darker,
the light of the Gospel shines ever brighter."[1]*

FRANKLIN GRAHAM

God is not limited by the darkness of the world. The Master does his best
work by shining light into the darkness.

My marriage had been one of little conflict. The divorce was something else. There was conflict over visitation, money, and parenting.
Before one argument passed, a new one would arise. Wounds opened
and reopened. We sniped at each other over the phone and through our
attorneys. Some battles were necessary. Some were based on the assump-
tion that the other side's motives could only be wrong.

Trying to forgive became an uphill climb in heavy rain, bitter cold, and dark fear when I did not see God's hand leading me to light. It would have been easy to give in to hate. To give up may have set hatred in my heart forever.

Human beings are complex. Most of our motivations, even the noble ones meant to benefit others rather than ourselves, are also complex. "All the ways of a man are clean in his own sight, but the LORD weighs the motives," the proverb says.[2] The Holy Spirit knows what moves us better than we do. Our motives may spring from a desire to honor God, to make an impression on others, to gain the feeling of having done something noble, or to be a vengeful victor. Sometimes all those motivations are wrapped up in one situation—in one ongoing set of situations. Many of my motivations centered on fear. I feared losing my children forever. My pride feared the label of "bad mother."

With few exceptions, divorce adds stress. One person now carries responsibilities meant for two—children, finances, home maintenance, car repair, the ordinary tasks of daily life. There is the emotional wound of rejection for one spouse and perhaps guilt for the other. Emotional wounds add fuel to the fire of other conflicts. Arguments over children and money continue for years after the ink has dried on the court documents.

Our culture stands on new and rapidly shifting ground since the sixties when the gay rights movement began as a fringe and marginal whisper. The whisper has increased its volume so gradually that we hardly saw it coming. Now that voice is shouting, and we seem stunned to see its influence and power to imperil our freedom of conscience.

As with any other issue we face today, we have a choice about how we will respond. Those who disagree with us are eager to accuse us of taking a "culture war" approach. If we come out fighting and bloody our opponents with our words, we will end up bleeding ourselves and lose any hope to regain the soul of our nation.

There are a couple ways to keep losing on this issue. One is to ignore it, pretending that all is well. Another is to react with anger and bitterness, etching the perception on the hearts and minds of those who don't even know us that we are hateful bigots.

There is a better way. In every encounter with those who disagree with us, we are always to act in love, accepting and respecting the sacred humanity of every person. But we are not to crumble under the pressure to endorse actions we cannot deem morally justified. More than any other issue, the homosexual controversy prompts us to "love the sinner and hate the sin." Many Christians have been far from loving while quick to condemn.

It's sad that those who assert that homosexual behavior is not sin can often point to pertinent Bible passages better than many Christians can. Ironically, the passage they seem to quote most often is from Leviticus: "You shall not lie with a male as one lies with a female; it is an abomination."[3] That statement seems clearly opposed to homosexual behavior. But many who cite this lump it in with other Old Testament rules that Christians disregard today. We don't keep kosher kitchens. We don't wear prayer shawls. We don't mark the Sabbath on Saturday. The implication is that sexual taboos are passé like the dietary laws of the past and not worthy of argument in our modern times.

Our critics also direct us to the Gospels where Jesus did not directly speak against homosexuality. They overlook the lack of disagreement within the Jewish community over the issue in that day. Jews then did not question the immorality of homosexual behavior. Further, Jesus was not one to avoid hot topics. In fact, he made many controversial statements when he walked the earth. Had he intended to approve same-sex marriage in a Jewish setting opposed to it, it's reasonable to expect that he would have done so explicitly.

Jesus performed his first public miracle at a wedding, one at which a man and a woman joined their lives. His affirmation of traditional marriage was positive. But even without a more direct statement from Jesus, the apostle Paul reaffirms the Old Testament perspective.

> We also know that the law is made not for the righteous but for lawbreakers and rebels, the ungodly and sinful, the unholy and irreligious, for those who kill their fathers or mothers, for murderers, for the sexually immoral, for those practicing homosexuality, for slave traders and liars and perjurers—and for whatever else is contrary to the sound doctrine that conforms to the gospel concerning the glory of the blessed God, which he entrusted to me.[4]

The rules regarding a kosher kitchen ended when God told Peter to "Rise ... kill and eat" meat previously forbidden to observant Jews.[5] The dietary rules had changed. The moral law did not.

With so many Christians being dragged into court to defend their convictions, it's natural for us to feel threatened. Lawsuits and court decisions are the reality that threatens our freedom. And we are right to defend ourselves. However, we must admit that our own responses have frequently played a part in forming the impression that we are hateful bigots regarding same-sex sin. While perception isn't always reality, it's influential. We simply haven't done all we could to show that our views originate in love. "It is not lost on the gay community that the church held no (or at least very few) marches or rallies against no-fault divorce, adultery, or other things that have done greater harm to marriage and families [than gay marriage has]," argues Ed Stetzer.[6]

According to Sam Allberry, Christians tend to not "treat homosexuality like other sins rather than treating [it] more seriously."

> Often, we treat homosexuality as if it's a kind of self-contained issue on its own, and we don't quite know what to do with it because we're not anchoring it in what the gospel tells us to do. Jesus says all of us need to repent and believe the gospel ... .
>
> Marriage is the joining together of like and unlike to reflect the marriage of Christ and the church. We believe what we do about homosexuality because of what we believe about marriage. When we talk about marriage, we will soon be talking about the gospel.[7]

Allberry is a strong voice on this issue because of his own struggle with same-sex attraction. He pastors a church in England and credits his congregation for being "supportive" and "an encouragement." His struggle "is not the lens through which they view me. [They feel that] we've all got our issues; this one is yours."[8]

For many Christians today, the controversy between LGBT customers and Christian businesses, such as florists, bakers, and wedding planners, is the face of this cultural challenge. There is another face, though, and many churches have too long ignored it. Allberry is that face. And he suggests some steps churches can take to effectively minister to those with same-sex attraction.

Creating a safe environment to discuss *any* temptation is the first step. A safe environment provides a place where we can express our challenges without fear of rejection. Such a place hosts a transparent community that can discuss *all* temptations—because it's not that God calls us to heterosexuality; it's that he calls us to *holiness*.[9] Being sexually active outside the traditional marriage relationship is sin. Rage is sin. Gluttony is sin. *Holiness* is our pursuit.[10] And we are to be the church that welcomes all wounded souls, all weary sinners.

Along with making the admission of same-sex attraction a safe subject for ministry, churches can do more to honor singleness as well. Celebrating a biblical understanding of sexual identity—that God made me who I am and did not make a mistake by giving me the wrong gender—is crucial.

Most importantly, Allberry says, the key to an effective ministry is creating an atmosphere of family—of "soul to soul" relationships. "The way we will most gain credibility is if people see those struggling with same-sex attraction in our churches flourishing far better than they would have in the gay community."[11]

As we must work to create an accepting yet truthful environment, the hostility toward our "bigoted" view of same-sex marriage increases. And some Christians are finding themselves in hot water for violating the most recent definition of bigotry. It's the claim that bigotry includes refusing to deem same-sex relationships good and morally sound. It's also the claim that bigotry includes refusing to acknowledge the perceived sexual identity of transgender people. Stewing in that hot water are some Christian teachers and business people—not just those who refuse to participate in same-sex weddings.

Our response to these situations must never involve anger or a desire for retribution. But that's a tall order for anyone in danger of losing the fruit of a lifetime of work.

As of this writing, that's what Barronelle Stutzman stands to lose: her floral business and her home in Washington State after refusing to provide flowers for a same-sex wedding. This case is in the appeal process, but there is also a fine detail to this story. Stutzman could have saved her assets by paying a settlement and promising never to "discriminate" again.

Washington's attorney general offered her the chance to settle the case and put the ordeal behind her for $2,001. Stutzman refused the offer. She said:

> Washington's constitution guarantees us "freedom of conscience in all matters of religious sentiment." I cannot sell that precious freedom. You are asking me to walk in the way of a well-known betrayer, one who sold something of infinite worth for 30 pieces of silver. That is something I will not do. ...

> Your offer reveals that you don't really understand me or what this conflict is all about. It's about freedom, not money. ... I certainly don't relish the idea of losing my business, my home, and everything else that your lawsuit threatens to take from my family, but my freedom to honor God in doing what I do best is more important.

Not the only floral shop in town, Stutzman's customer had been free to shop elsewhere over the years they had done business together. Not only had Stutzman regularly served members of the LGBT community for many years, she had also employed them.[12] She is hardly a bigot.

There are those even within orthodoxy who would encourage Stutzman to give in. They say that Jesus would encourage her to provide the flowers, bakers to bake the cakes, and planners to plan the ceremonies. Such a philosophy blurs the lines between maintaining a positive Christian testimony and caving in to an appeal to force—a threat of "come along, or else!" And it makes no room for Christians to follow their conscience. It also means we will be no different from the rest of the world who pretend there is no sin except the sin of intolerance. This view demands that we adopt the pretense that there are no consequences for sin. Those powers pressuring Stutzman to discard her beliefs would prefer to present her as a reformed bigot—someone who paid her small fine and learned her lesson. By standing her ground, she stands on principle rather than expedience.

And if she loses the fruit of her lifelong labors, will she still be a bigot? Or will she then become more of a victim than those she supposedly victimized herself? In light of her persecution, some opponents may change their perception of her from that of a hateful person to a martyr of sorts. Win or lose, she will be the one who risked all her worldly wealth for a biblical standard that can never change.

Those who encourage her to give in may assume that florists, bakers, and wedding planners are the endgame. They ignore the next step that will most assuredly take place within our own sanctuaries. Given the 2015 US Supreme Court *Obergefell* decision approving same-sex marriage throughout the US, whether we might expect heavy-handed treatment remains to be seen.

The 2018 *Masterpiece Cakeshop vs. Colorado Civil Rights Commission* decision is a case in point. Justice Anthony Kennedy authored the majority opinion for this case. Kennedy has since announced his retirement. But when the decision came down, some saw his opinion as a signal of his "future support for religious conservatives."[13] However, Darel E. Paul disagreed with the idea that *Masterpiece* was a conservative win. "The Court majority ruled in favor of Phillips strictly on procedural grounds. The substance of his claim to refuse to bake custom cakes for same-sex weddings went untested. In fact, the balance of the five separate opinions filed by the nine justices strongly suggests that the next *Masterpiece Cakeshop* will not fare nearly so well."[14]

As I write, the nation waits for President Trump to announce his nominee to replace Kennedy. In the meantime, the partisan sides in the Senate are lining up for battle. The next Supreme Court justice may be a tipping point on the court, holding religious freedom and other concerns in the balance while subsequent *Masterpiece Cakeshop* cases are already litigating in the wings.

In the meantime, there are questions Christians should consider. Will those of us who say that Jesus would have us bake the cake also say that Jesus would have us provide our altars for same-sex ceremonies? And if we do not give in then, the next appeal to force may mean the loss of tax-exempt status for churches that will not comply. Will threats go beyond financial sanction? Can we have any assurance they won't?

The largest challenge of this debate will be to exhibit love toward those who would attack the mere expression of an orthodox view. That happens when we speak truth in love—as Barronelle Stutzman has. It happens when we respond as Christ did, forgiving those who know not what they do. It happens when we pay a price and do so graciously.

That is when Christ's light shines through darkness as a distinct picture. Some will refuse to look at the image. But some will see the image of the window and find their way to the light.

No stumbling pilgrim in the dark,
The road to Zion's in your heart.[15]

Mike Hudson

{ENDNOTES}

1   Franklin Graham, "The Light Shines in the Darkness," Billy Graham Evangelistic Association, January 5, 2011, https://billygraham.org/decision-magazine/january-2011/the-light-shines-in-the-darkness.

2   Proverbs 16:2.

3   Leviticus 18:22.

4   1 Timothy 1:8–11, NIV.

5   Acts 10:13.

6   Ed Stetzer, "Evangelicals and Same-Sex Marriage: An Interview with John Stonestreet and Sean McDowell," *Christianity Today*, August 27, 2014, https://www.christianitytoday.com/edstetzer/2014/august/evangelicals-and-same-sex-marriage-interview-with-john-ston.html.

7   Sam Allberry, as quoted in RuthAnn Irvine, "Churches Essential in Ministry to Those with Same-Sex Attraction, Allberry Says in Lecture," The Southern Baptist Theological Seminary, March 11, 2015, http://news.sbts.edu/2015/03/11/churches-essential-in-ministry-to-those-with-same-sex-attraction-allberry-says-in-lecture.

8   Sam, "Sam's Story," *Living Out*, video bio, accessed April 28, 2015, http://www.livingout.org/stories/sam.

9   Bob Allen, "Speakers Say Holiness, Not Heterosexuality, Goal of Outreach to Gays," *Baptist News*, October 29, 2014, https://baptistnews.com/article/speakers-say-holiness-not-heterosexuality-goal-of-outreach-to-gays/#.WyFin-4vzIU.

10 Rick Noen, "Same-Sex Attraction and the Wait for Change," *Desiring God*, January 29, 2014, https://www.desiringgod.org/articles/same-sex-attraction-and-the-wait-for-change.

11 Stetzer, "Evangelicals and Same-Sex Marriage."

12 Samuel Smith, "Florist Who Refused Gay Wedding Offered Settlement: I Will Not Be Like Judas, Betray Jesus for Money, She Replied," *Christian Post*, February 23, 2015, https://www.christianpost.com/news/florist-who-refused-gay-wedding-offered-settlement-i-will-not-be-like-judas-betray-jesus-for-money-she-replied-134593.

13 David French, "In *Masterpiece Cakeshop*, Justice Kennedy Stikes a Blow for the Dignity of the Faithful," *National Review*, June 4, 2018, https://www.nationalreview.com/2018/06/masterpiece-cakeshop-ruling-religious-liberty-victory.

14 Darel E. Paul, "No Victory for Religious Liberty," *First Things*, June 5, 2018, https://www.firstthings.com/web-exclusives/2018/06/no-victory-for-religious-liberty.

15 Mike Hudson, "The Road to Zion," Straightway Music, CCLI, 1982.

Sixteen
THE CHILDREN OF BROKENNESS

"Moab is broken, Her little ones have sounded out a cry of distress."

JEREMIAH 48:4

_"Hearts can get really fragile, don't they? I felt like
mine was made of thin glass—easily picked up but also
easily broken. Vulnerability came easy for me when I was younger,
until the thin glass started to break little by little."[1]_

CATHY C.

Two months after I graduated from college—and a few weeks after the financial crisis that had emptied our kitchen cupboards—I started a job in the newsroom of a local news/talk radio station. My job was challenging and exciting but very part-time. Gradually my hours increased. By March of the following year, I was working full-time. I learned hand over fist about the radio business and about local news issues, covering public meetings, political campaigns, and crime reports. I learned how to interview people, which questions to ask, and how to incorporate quotes into news stories suitable for short newscasts. Eventually, I was producing the morning drive program and filling in occasionally as a co-host. The people I worked with were seasoned professionals, gracious enough to invest their time in a novice.

Radio news was exhilarating, but the hours were long and not particularly family friendly. One evening, the children and I were decorating our Christmas tree when I was called to cover a fire—arson suspected. Our memory-making moments for the evening had come to an end.

Small market radio jobs aren't famous for good pay. I took the first $100 I could spare, probably from an income tax credit, and set up a savings account for overdraft protection. Every payday, I tried to get to the bank before the checks I had already mailed could get there. I was running as fast as I could to get nowhere.

The children spent one or two evenings a week with a babysitter or, as they grew, by themselves, while I covered public meetings. It was common for me to come home after they were already asleep.

Divorce is hardest on children. Brokenness always accompanies divorce—especially for the children. There are broken hearts and fragmented loyalties, unmet needs, and fear. Perhaps the most visible ill resulting from divorce is increased poverty. Children who live with single parents (be they mothers or fathers) are much more likely to live in poverty.[2] Families headed by single mothers are seven times more likely to be living in poverty than intact families, but the problems divorced or unmarried families face go much deeper than poverty.[3]

The fallout from couples divorcing or cohabiting often finds children bouncing between their parents' homes or eventually losing all contact with one parent, most often Dad. And even though teen pregnancies are down considerably, 36 percent of US births in 2013 were to unwed parents.[4] By 2016, the rate was nearly 40 percent.[5] The reasons these statistics are important are innumerable. One bad situation at home can lead to a multitude of bad possibilities that wound children's spirits and make life even more difficult. Of course, not all children of divorce or unmarried relationships suffer all these ills, and children from intact families are not immune to them. But children in single parent homes face greater peril.

Children who live in single parent, low-income families are at greater risk of sexual abuse than their peers from higher income, intact families.[6] They are also more likely to drop out of school and experience a teen pregnancy (continuing a pattern of brokenness). Boys who grow up in a single parent family are twice as likely to be arrested by age thirty as their peers from intact families.[7]

Avoiding single parenthood by opting for unmarried cohabitation may pull the family out of the frying pan and land them right in the fire. The damage done, particularly to children whose single parents choose unwise alliances, is incalculable. Without emotional support and reliable financial support, single mothers often flounder and can be prey to men who abuse them or their children or both. Financial burdens, difficulties with children, and feelings of rejection or loneliness are just some of the reasons single mothers enter cohabiting relationships.

Whether their mothers remain alone, remarry, or decide to cohabit, many children lose all contact with their fathers after a divorce or separation. Some are deadbeat dads; others are "ghost dads"—men who pay support but see their children seldom or never. These men often can't resolve their feelings over the loss of their families or manage ongoing conflict with their ex-wives or ex-partners. They can't elude the sense that a stepfather replaced them or navigate the complexities of a job relocation for either former spouse.[8] As decades of high divorce rates roll along, it's likely that many of today's deadbeat and ghost dads suffered a similar abandonment in their own youth, again continuing a pattern of brokenness.

Even so, while some men are walking away, others are taking on the role of single parent. But these families have their challenges too. The number of single parent households headed by men is nine times what it was in 1960, with 2.6 million households led by single dads (24 percent of single parent households).[9] Single dads are less likely than single mothers to have flexible work hours. These fathers are less likely than single moms to receive financial support (but also less likely to need it).[10] Yet they still do not fare as well as married couples. They are more likely than their female counterparts to be cohabiting, and those who are cohabiting are more likely to live in poverty than single fathers who live without a partner.[11] Seventy-five percent of all divorced people eventually remarry. Men remarry more often than women do. Those men tend to have weaker relationships and less contact with their adult children than men who have never divorced.[12] Weakened relationships mean more cracked glass.

And while single moms cohabit at a lower rate than single dads do, it's still very common for a single mom to have a live-in boyfriend.[13] A cohabiting partner might provide emotional support—the reassurance that she is worthy of his attention, if not his commitment. He may also contribute financially. But he does not typically contribute to the emotional wellbeing of her children.

It doesn't matter whether the cohabiting parent is mom or dad or both partners are the child's parents. Even such unmarried relationships free of abuse are not beneficial. In a best case scenario when children and their cohabiting parent (male or female) get along well, more likely than not, the situation sets up kids for the disappointment of more separation and loss since half of all cohabiters are no longer together after five years. The picture is bleaker still for children born into cohabiting situations. More than 75 percent of children born to unmarried parents will no longer live with both parents by the time the child reaches age fifteen.[14]

I know a family who fostered two young boys with a history of neglect and abuse. The boys are the oldest two siblings of eight children. They have different fathers as do the remaining six siblings with whom they share a mother. Adults form and break such bonds regularly today. With every such break, children become more wounded and less able to form their own healthy bonds later on. When wounded people reach out to the church for help, we can create fresh wounds or we can foster healing. Here are two examples.

"Katie" and her live-in boyfriend began to attend church. The couple had a young child, and they planned to get married "someday." At church, they seemed to fit in nicely with other couples their age, but at a church gathering, a "Christian" woman informed Katie that she would never be able to join the church since she was living with her boyfriend and her child had been born out of wedlock. She seemed to have no concern for Katie's soul—just rejection—declaring that we have a club and you can't join. Had Katie and her boyfriend asked to become members of the church, it would have been appropriate for the pastor to counsel them privately.

She and her boyfriend quit going to church.

In the second example, a young mother, let's call her "Emma," rode the church bus one summer with her two young children so they could attend vacation Bible school. During the program, Emma hung out in the church kitchen where volunteers were preparing snacks for the children. That's where Emma met "Jim"—an elder of the church. Jim befriended Emma, engaged her in conversation, and encouraged her to commit her life to Christ. Emma accepted the invitation and, at the end of the evening, went home to her live-in boyfriend.

Jim and other church members were happy about Emma's faith commitment but sad that she continued in her live-in situation. Sad but silent. Emma kept coming to church with her children. Members welcomed them; teachers nurtured them.

Within weeks, Emma broke up with her boyfriend and established her own home. She and the children became faithful members of the church. Eventually, Emma married the church bus driver, and the two continue to live faithfully today.

Emma's community welcomed her and loved her. While they were not comfortable with her situation, they didn't interfere as the Holy Spirit worked in her heart. By attending church, she and her children could meet intact families and see examples of faithful marriages that they may not have had the opportunity to observe before. Faithfulness breeds faithfulness. Instability breeds instability.

Children do not move from one loose connection to the next with the same apparent ease adults seem to show. I was very surprised to discover how little it takes for kids to form a connection with a potential father figure. In the summer before I began taking college classes, I briefly dated a very nice man (let's call him "Bill") who turned out not to be the right person for our family. He was cordial, handsome, well educated, and made a nice income, but he didn't believe in God. *Maybe*, I thought, *he will come to see the light.*

Most of our dates occurred when my children were with their father, so their exposure to Bill was limited. They did meet him. He seemed to like them, and they seemed to like him. But by autumn, the relationship with Bill fizzled.

The next summer, I enrolled Chris in Instructional Baseball, a step up from T-ball but not yet Little League. One day, we got to the field and Chris realized he had forgotten his mitt. It was a short drive home, but

Chris wasn't exactly sure where he had put the mitt and how long it would take him to find it. That is stress to a seven-year-old. Then Chris asked me a question that seemed to have flown in from the great blue beyond.

"Mommy, why didn't you marry Bill?"

I had to pause. "He wasn't the right one."

Chris was quiet for the rest of the ride home—either processing my answer or pondering where the mitt might be. Once home, we found the mitt quickly and returned to a nice morning at the field. I'm not sure why his mind went back to that relationship after so much time had passed, but I realized that the little bit of exposure he had to a guy I had briefly dated had churned in his imagination for months afterward.

Chris seems to have acquired no great wound from this experience, but imagine if the relationship had become serious—if it had gone on for years instead of months—if we had all lived together and then separated—if there had been other "Bills." More Bills would have meant more cracks in Chris' glass, and larger ones.

I had made the easier choice before my first marriage. That decision led to our difficult times. Part of my family was gone and the ones who remained with me lived in poverty. Then I committed myself to the hard choice of waiting for intentional love. I had no idea how hard that wait would be. This time I wanted to rely on God to help me make the right choice. The cost of making the wrong one had been high, and the cost of making a bad choice twice would only cause more pain that would reverberate through generations. More broken glass.

But in the real world, you couldn't really just split a family down the middle, mom on one side, dad the other, with the child equally divided between. It was like when you ripped a piece of paper into two: no matter how you tried, the seams never fit exactly right again. It was what you couldn't see, those tiniest of pieces, that were lost in the severing, and their absence kept everything from being complete.[15]

SARAH DESSEN

{Endnotes}

1   Cathy C., "Forgiveness and a Fragile Heart: A Faith Barista Jam," *Periwinkle Confessions* (blog), February 24, 2011, https://periwinkleconfessions. blogspot.com/search?q=faith+and+a+fragile+heart.

2   Josh Mitchell, "About Half of Kids with Single Moms Live in Poverty," *The Wall Street Journal*, November 25, 2013, https://blogs.wsj.com/ economics/2013/11/25/about-half-of-kids-with-single-moms-live-in-poverty.

3   Shanta Pandey et al, "Bachelor's Degree for Women with Children: A Promising Pathway to Poverty Reduction," Equal Opportunities International, *Proquest*, 2006, accessed March 13, 2014, https://search-proquest-com. ezaccess.libraries.psu.edu/docview/199620794?pq-origsite=summon&acco untid=13158.

4   US Department of Health and Human Services, "Trends in Teen Pregnancy and Childbearing," accessed June 13, 2018, https://www.hhs.gov/ash/ oah/adolescent-development/reproductive-health-and-teen-pregnancy/ teen-pregnancy-and-childbearing/trends/index.html; Christina Huffington, "Single Motherhood Increases Dramatically for Certain Demographics, Census Bureau Reports," *Huffington Post*, May 2, 2013, https://www. huffingtonpost.com/2013/05/01/single-motherhood-increases-census-report_n_3195455.html.

5   Centers for Disease Control and Prevention, "Percentage of Births to Unmarried Mothers by State," accessed February 20, 2018, https://www.cdc. gov/nchs/pressroom/sosmap/unmarried/unmarried.htm.

6   William C. Holmes, as quoted in "One-Parent Households Double Risk of Childhood Sexual Abuse," *Science Daily*, University of Pennsylvania School of Medicine, March 14, 2007, https://www.sciencedaily.com/ releases/2007/03/070313114303.htm.

7   Pandey et al, "Bachelor's Degree for Women with Children."

8   Hossein Berenji, "6 Reasons Some Divorced Dads Check out of Their Children's Lives," The Good Men Project, May 25, 2016, https:// goodmenproject.com/featured-content/6-reasons-some-divorced-dads-check-out-of-their-childrens-lives-dg.

9   Gretchen Livingston, "The Rise of Single Fathers: A Ninefold Increase since 1960," Pew Research Center, July 2, 2013, http://www.pewsocialtrends. org/2013/07/02/the-rise-of-single-fathers.

10   Education.com, "Fathers Raising Daughters: The Unique Challenges of Single Fatherhood," May 4, 2011, https://www.education.com/magazine/article/Fathers_Raising_Daughters.

11   Livingston, "The Rise of Single Fathers."

12   *Huffington Post*, "Parent-Child Relationship Weakened by Fathers' Remarriage Post-Divorce (Study)," May 22, 2013, https://www.huffingtonpost.com/2013/05/22/parentchild-relationship-_n_3322633.html.

13   Livingston, "The Rise of Single Fathers."

14   Terry Gaspard, "Cohabitation with Children: What Are the Risks?," *Huffington Post*, September 12, 2013, https://www.huffingtonpost.com/terry-gaspard-msw-licsw/cohabitation-with-childre_b_3910608.html.

15   Sarah Dessen, *What Happened to Goodbye* (New York: Viking, 2011), 165.

Seventeen
BROKEN GLASS, BREAKING GLASS

*"[B]ut Jesus said, 'Let the little children come to me and do
not hinder them, for to such belongs the kingdom of heaven.'"*

Matthew 19:14 ESV

*"All parents damage their children. It cannot be helped.
Youth, like pristine glass absorbs the prints of its handlers.
Some parents smudge, others crack, a few shatter childhoods
completely into jagged little pieces, beyond repair."[1]*

Mitch Albom

It was a snapshot moment. We stood in the kitchen, not looking at each
other. She had decided.

Six weeks before her high school graduation, Angela left home
to live with a series of family members, finally moving in with an aunt
who had few rules. She chose neither her father nor me. She chose freedom—a person and a place from which she could do just about anything
she wanted. This decision looked to me like a bad choice leading in a
wrong direction.

Would the cracks in her glass keep accumulating? Or would she find a way to heal from wounds accumulated over the years?

Were the cracks in her glass beyond repair? Are anyone's ever?

At this point, only two children remained with me. I lived with the dread that someday, one or both of them would leave prematurely too.

There are several levels of separation between parents and children after divorce. Some kids split their time between two homes. Some spend more time with Mom or more with Dad. Some live with one parent and maintain healthy relationships with both.

A neighbor girl lived with her divorced mother. The girl and her brother had decided on their own that the brother would live with Dad and the sister with Mom so neither parent would be alone. But such arrangements don't always please everyone. And that's when battles begin. When one or both parents are angry, things can get ugly fast. But kids get angry too. Some children are mad at the parent who, either overtly or in the child's eyes, unilaterally caused the divorce. Some don't get along well with their new stepparent. To get what they want, most children (even in intact families), at one time or another, will play one parent against the other. It can take decades for the cracks of divorce to heal, if ever.

Many children suffer from parental alienation (PA). PA happens in varying degrees at three levels. The mildest level occurs when a child overhears one parent complaining about the other—even if the complaining parent didn't intend the child to hear. This parent wants the child to maintain a healthy relationship with the other parent but doesn't realize the consequences of such criticism.[2]

Many divorces, and many marriages for that matter, contain at least some alienation, even if it's infrequent. I knew my children needed a relationship with their father, and I encouraged that. But I didn't always guard my words as I should have. Now I understand that no parent should ever put any child in that position.

In a similar but more damaging vein, a parent operating at the moderate level of alienation also criticizes the other parent but makes no effort to conceal his or her anger. In such cases, the child often takes steps to "protect" the alienating parent and will "stop expressing positive feelings for the target parent" to keep the alienator from exploding. In this scenario, the alienating parent causes anguish for both the child (who cannot understand what's really happening) and the "target" parent.[3]

But there is another level of alienation that's much worse. In the "severe" category of alienation, one parent actively pursues "trying to destroy the child's relationship with the other parent and that parent's family and friends." This kind of parent is "disturbed." Every person has cracks in their glass, but severe alienators are broken glass who cannot stop themselves from shattering others. "Often people who exhibit this level of nastiness have come from a disastrously dysfunctional family or have experienced a serious trauma that went untreated. They are unreasonably demanding and resist any discussion or negotiation to make a situation better. They must have their way and are rigid about expecting others to comply with what they want."[4] Alienating parents often have a "borderline or antisocial personality disorder, as well as being active alcoholics."[5]

Getting children to side with one parent confirms what that parent already believes: *I am good and the other is bad.* Whether it's sports, the presidential election, or our own families, we all enjoy having more people on our side. But this situation goes beyond winning and losing. It's about controlling.

A disturbed parent can have a remarkable level of success in alienating a child—and do a great deal of damage. One researcher asserts that effective treatment for alienation includes methods used to "deprogram individuals involved in cults."[6] That's because alienating parents use "emotional manipulation and thought reform strategies" that cults use to influence followers. Children who grow up in such drastic situations can suffer a multitude of problems, including an "inability to make rational choices," "serious psychiatric disorders," and "poor social relationships." Alienation is "a form of abuse that damages the child's self-esteem in the short run and is associated with lifelong damage."[7]

It doesn't help that, in any antagonistic divorce, counselors, attorneys, and judges find it difficult to sort out the reality of the situation. Some parents cause alienation and make false allegations of abuse. But some parents do abuse children. And a manipulated child can sometimes be just as convincing as an otherwise abused one.

Growing awareness of PA can help judges and others involved to determine which kind of abuse is happening—the kind we've understood for a long time or another kind, PA, we are just coming to understand.[8] Because the legal system is adversarial, one parent will win and another will lose in cases like these. But an alienated child cannot win unless everyone involved realizes the truth that one parent is alienating and the other is victimized.

Alienation is shattered glass shattering the future.

Bonnie Gray was the child of alienation. Her father left when she was young, but she was old enough to remember him leaving. Her mother worked very hard to destroy every vestige of positive memory of her father. She forced Bonnie to tear up his pictures and controlled every aspect of Bonnie's life—where she went to college, even what she would study.

As a married adult with two children, Bonnie's problems appeared to be behind her. Her husband was loving, her children healthy. She had found faith in Christ. But Bonnie began to have panic attacks, bad dreams, and sleepless nights. Her therapist told her she had post-traumatic-stress-disorder (PTSD). Bonnie explains: "PTSD often surfaces in people in their thirties and forties—when major life changes are occurring. The stresses we've hidden deep inside finally emerge when we can no longer bolt down what we fear the most—*our wounded selves*."[9]

Cracks in the glass remain stagnant, perhaps for decades. Then life changes and the cracks emerge to illustrate pain that has lingered beneath the surface all along. Such wounds don't heal themselves.

Bonnie struggled in the aftermath of her mother's abuse. She worked with a therapist, battling the past, yearning to move beyond. She had to face the demons of her past. But she also found relief in what she called whitespace—in resting and ministering to herself. Therapy helped, but healing took a long time.

The therapy she participated in is one way to treat child alienation.[10] Therapy helps people understand and change how they think about the trauma they've suffered. A therapist helps the traumatized understand the way they think about situations in their past and how that way of thinking causes them stress. Then they can begin to think about painful events of the past in a new way. They can change how they react to painful memories.

Of course, this therapy must happen in a safe place—where adult or child can share freely.[11]

We tend not to think of the separation within the church as alienation. But that (minus the trauma, we hope) is what happens when one believer teaches another a distortion about a different tradition. Younger generations inherit distortions that build walls of fear and distrust. They destroy the possibility of accord.

A widely accepted evangelical distortion of Catholicism claims that the Roman Church is the false church that will lead many astray during the end times. This view is deeply entrenched in the thinking of many fundamentalist Christians, the most conservative of Protestant evangelicals.

As a young evangelist, Ralph Woodrow authored a book, *Babylon Mystery Religion,* promoting this view based on the teachings of Alexander Hislop (1807–1862). Woodrow's book became popular and was translated into several languages. He encountered only a few who disagreed with him.

One of those few was Scott Klemm, a Christian high school history teacher, who questioned Hislop's lack of scholarship on which Woodrow had heavily relied.[12] Klemm's criticism prompted Woodrow to look into Hislop's research more deeply. After investigating Hislop's assertions further, Woodrow found them to be "wild speculation" and "nonsense."[13] At the end of his analysis, Woodrow's viewpoint had shifted to conclude that, while there are "distinct differences ... in doctrine, interpretation, and emphasis," Catholicism and evangelicalism "hold a number of *major* beliefs in common."[14]

Without leaving the realm of evangelical doctrine, Woodrow now proposes that "[i]nstead of using a sweeping statement that the Roman Catholic Church (or some other group) is wrong on 'all' it teaches, it would be better to find areas of agreement, establish some common ground, and build from there."[15] Woodrow points to Luke 9 when Christ's disciples saw someone ministering in Jesus' name, but they "rejected him because he did not belong to our group." Christ chided them not to reject him for " 'he who is not against us is for us' ... emphasizing the principle of inclusion, not exclusion."[16] Woodrow still rejects certain Catholic doctrines but admonishes his readers not to "shun those who may have come from a different denominational background. This is not compromise, but compassion."[17] This compassion, should we demonstrate it, can change the hearts and minds of many who have negative views of our faith.

We can pick up the pieces and help the window become whole again. We can consider what we learned in the past and begin to think in a new way. When we do, fewer people will be drawn into alienation against other Christians or against Christianity itself. Then, for many, authentic healing can begin.

*Has it ever occurred to you that one hundred
pianos all tuned to the same fork are
automatically tuned to each other? They are of
one accord by being tuned, not to each other,
but to another standard to which each one must
individually bow.*[18]

A. W. TOZER

{Endnotes}

1   Mitch Albom, *The Five People You Meet in Heaven* (New York: Hachette Books, 2003), 104.

2   Jane A. Major, "Parental Alienation Syndrome (PAS): Its Causes, Cures, Costs, and Controversies," Major Family Services, accessed July 7, 2016, http://www.majorfamilyservices.com/parental-alienation-syndrome-pas-its-causes-cures-costs-and-controversies.html.

3   Ibid.

4   Ibid.

5   Amy J. L. Baker, "Parental Alienation Is Emotional Abuse for Children," *Psychology Today*, June 28, 2011, https://www.psychologytoday.com/us/blog/caught-between-parents/201106/parental-alienation-is-emotional-abuse-children.

6   Major, "Parental Alienation Syndrome (PAS)."

7   Baker, "Parental Alienation Is Emotional Abuse."

8   Dr. Richard Warshak, "What Judges Need to Know in Parental Alienation Cases," *Plutoverse*, January 10, 2011, http://warshak.com/blog/2011/01/10/what-judges-need-to-know-in-parental-alienation-cases.

9   Bonnie Gray, *Finding Spiritual White Space: Awakening Your Soul to Rest* (Grand Rapids: Revell, 2014), 38, Gray's emphasis.

10 Benjamin D. Garber, "Cognitive Behavioral Methods in High-Conflict Divorce: Systematic Desensitization Adapted to Parent-Child Reunification Interventions," *Family Court Review*, vol. 53, no. 1 (January 2015), 96–112, Wiley Online, https://onlinelibrary-wiley-com.ezaccess.libraries.psu.edu/doi/epdf/10.1111/fcre.12133.

11 National Center for PTSD, "Treatment of PTSD," US Department of Veterans Affairs, accessed July 13, 2016, https://www.ptsd.va.gov/public/treatment/therapy-med/treatment-ptsd.asp.

12 Ralph Woodrow, *The Babylon Connection?* (Palm Springs: Ralph Woodrow Evangelistic Association, 1997), Introduction.

13 Ibid., 18, 20.

14 Ibid., 112, Woodrow's emphasis.

15 Ibid., 111.

16 Ibid., 119–20. See also Luke 9:49–50.

17   Ibid., 120.

18   A. W. Tozer, *The Pursuit of God: The Human Thirst for the Divine*, Goodreads, accessed June 1, 2018, https://www.goodreads.com/quotes/369949-has-it-ever-occurred-to-you-that-one-hundred-pianos.

Eighteen
A CANDLE IN THE WINDOW

"The night is far gone; the day is at hand. So then let us cast off the works of darkness and put on the armor of light."

ROMANS 13:12 ESV

"Look at how a single candle can both defy and define the darkness."[1]

ANNE FRANK

When I was a new high school student in Pennsylvania, a young man in New England was having an adventure. It would be years before we would meet. We could never have imagined the wilderness we each would travel. Nor could we foresee that someday our paths would cross, merge into one, and lead us to the same desire to help those in need and to pursue Christian accord.

When Paul was a teenager, he experienced homelessness when an incredible situation unfolded in Massachusetts during the raucous days of his teen years. He had been sleeping in a friend's farm stand because of a dispute with his parents over the length of his hair. On September 20, 1970, he was walking from the farm stand to school. It was a day that seemed as unremarkable as any other. Then he reached the Newburyport

Armory. A bit of a mad scientist, fascinated with things that go bang, make smoke, or have already ignited, he stopped to watch the flashes of fire emerging from the building. He paused. A crowd gathered. The police arrived.

In the 1970s, long hair donned by young men indicated more than self-expression. Then it was a signpost of rebellion. At that time, some adults might surmise that a longhaired teenage boy could be a revolutionary subversive. But it was more likely for the longhaired teenage boy to assume the police would deem him responsible for mischief anywhere in his proximity. Having participated in some protest efforts that produced a police response, Paul drew precisely that conclusion. When the police asked who in the group of spectators had been first on the scene, a good citizen pointed to Paul and said, "He was."

Paul stopped fleeing when he reached Flagstaff, Arizona. That's where the police caught up with him. It hadn't taken them long to realize that the domestic terrorist group the Weathermen was behind the raid, theft of heavy armaments, and arson in Newburyport. In Flagstaff, however, Paul was just a runaway kid who thought he was eluding a bogus rap.

As he traveled across the country, he often scavenged for food in dumpsters. Sometimes he would sit in a McDonalds and wait for a mother with a not so hungry tot. If the child refused to eat, Paul would offer to take the remains of the meal to keep her from throwing it away. In Flagstaff, he hitched a ride with a Christian who invited him to a Bible study—a spark offered to fuse cracked glass. The ignition of faith would come later.

The police in Flagstaff put Paul on a bus back to Massachusetts to reunite him with his anxious parents. He extended his journey when he failed to get back on the bus before it departed from Tulsa, Oklahoma. He was getting a haircut.

His amazing odyssey seared into his being what it means to not have enough money to eat and to be uncertain when the next meal will come. His adventure delayed his education for a year, but he was fortunate to return to a stable family situation and finish high school before joining the army.

Later, because of his military service, the GI Bill provided the cost of his college education. While the situation that caused his homelessness was unusual, so was his outcome. College graduation is not a typical result for homeless youths.

Upon his return to Massachusetts, compassionate Christians showed him how to become part of the window. His placement there would mend old cracks and be a salve to later ones. Along his way, he carried memories of hunger and homelessness.

Two decades after his westward journey, Paul was forecasting weather as part of a team working on international hot air balloon projects. The team spent some time in poverty-ridden Nepal. On the ground outside the entrance to their hotel sat an old woman. She was unbathed and dressed in a ragged sari and headscarf. She used her skirt to collect the proceeds of a day's begging efforts. As the patrons entered and exited, she was there every day raising her hand to ask for rupees and smiling weakly upon receiving a small gift. That place on the ground was her home.

During the team's stay, a revolution ensued, and one morning, Paul exited the building to find the woman had died there on the sidewalk—right on the doorstep of relative wealth. He wasn't sure whether she was a war casualty or had died of starvation.

When I was a child, my parents told me to clean my plate because "a starving child in China would love to have that food." In my young mind, starving Chinese children were not real, and I would have gladly shared all the food I didn't like. As an adult, Paul understood that the Nepali woman was a human soul. Because of the imprint she made on his heart, he works hard not to waste food.

Recently, I was soaking in that wonderful feeling of being home at the end of a day, enjoying that sense of contentment that comes from the completion of a day's obligations. The thought struck me: *That's how heaven is going to feel. Coming home, being at home.* Even with frustrations over stalled improvement projects and the hassles of regular maintenance—there truly is no place like home. But for many in America today, home is a patch of sidewalk, a car, or an abandoned building, hardly places that would invite you to rejoice upon arrival.

When you do an online search for *home* in the scriptures, you find a variety of verses from Genesis to Titus, most presuming a home is something everyone has. In 1 Samuel, Elkanah and Hannah go home after delivering the recently dedicated Samuel to his new home, the temple. Jesus visits the home of Simon the leper. The apostle Paul admonishes the Corinthians to eat at home when they are hungry so they can keep the communion meal sacred.[2]

"Home," Robert Frost wrote, "is the place where, when you have to go there, / They have to take you in."[3]

Still, homelessness is not a modern development. Isaiah reminds us to fast so we have the means to help the homeless.[4] Moses, Jacob, Elijah, David, and Ruth all were homeless at some point. Jeremiah mourns Jerusalem's captive homelessness, an entire people yearning for the familiar consolation of home.[5] Paul points out his own homeless status to the Corinthians.[6] And while Jesus dwelled first in Nazareth, Egypt, and then in Capernaum,[7] his birth in a stable is akin to homelessness. Both Matthew and Luke provide the account of Jesus telling a prospective follower that he has "Nowhere to lay his head."[8]

Having a home means security and solace.

Lacking one means deprivation and trauma.

When Paul and I began to investigate the needs of people in our area, it became apparent that housing for the homeless is the biggest need here. While many areas see progress in reducing homelessness, a shortage of housing for the extremely poor looms in some areas.[9]

Nationwide, 8 percent of the homeless are vets.[10] But as many as 80 percent of them suffer from addiction or mental illness. Overall, about 20 percent of the homeless are mentally ill.[11] A 2008 survey by the United States Conference of Mayors found that substance abuse was the single largest cause of homelessness for single adults. However, some people become homeless because of addiction, and others become addicts because of homelessness.[12] Homelessness and hopelessness go hand in hand.

The financial cost of homelessness is untold. Homeless people seek their medical care in emergency rooms, which is more costly than routine medical care. They land in jail, sometimes intentionally to avoid harsh weather. They are seldom employed because of the issues that caused their homelessness.

They are ill, addicted, emotionally wounded, hopeless, or a combination of those factors. They lack transportation, marketable skills, and the means to maintain proper hygiene. Homelessness brings increased medical and correctional costs, lost tax revenues, and unearned dollars forever lost to our economy.

Most of all, it prevents the mending of shattered glass.

Everyone needs companionship and community, but not everyone will easily adapt to functioning well within a work community. The wounds from addiction and abuse often make social interaction difficult at best. Government's response has not always been compassionate or effective.

In 2007, Mayor Michael Bloomberg of New York pledged to reduce homelessness in the Big Apple as he "gave homeless people one-way tickets out of town, charged families for using emergency shelters and evicted people from these shelters who broke curfew ... . [Homelessness] rates subsequently rose 80% to become the highest since New York began keeping records 30 years ago."[13] The city's homelessness problem is even worse today.[14]

The financial cost of homelessness is only a reflection of the personal damage the problem represents. The trauma people suffer living on the streets compounds any abuse they suffered before they became homeless. The reverberation of their distress echoes through the years and into the next generation, whose members are even more likely to suffer ordeals costly to our neighborhoods and nation.

The mentally ill, those suffering from substance abuse, and traumatized veterans do not complete the ranks of the homeless. Forty percent of the homeless are under eighteen. And half of children who age out of foster care and the juvenile justice system will become homeless within six months of their eighteenth birthday. PTSD, drug problems, and mental illness are the causes we usually associate with homelessness, but divorce, abuse, job loss, physical illness, and even issues as minor as car problems can push people over the edge of their resources and onto the streets.[15]

For those who have recently become homeless, it would not take much to get them back on their feet. For these people, we can be companions.

Years ago, Anne was working in her office, a storefront pro-life presence near her home, when a young couple walked in and asked for help. They had spent the last of their resources to come to our city for a promised job that fell through. They found themselves without the means to obtain a place to live. Anne let the couple stay in her office while she worked on finding housing for them.

She paid the security deposit and first month's rent on an apartment and gave them some provisions until assistance benefits began. Eventually, the couple moved to a new area and found solid financial footing. Their problem was temporary, and Anne's companionship carried them through it. Her investment of some household supplies and two months' rent got this couple back into the mainstream of society.

Anne had long since grown from taking in lost puppies to housing unwed pregnant girls and sponsoring Vietnamese refugees. Over the years, she welcomed many road weary travelers into her home. When Paul first came to Altoona to meet me, he was a guest at Anne's house.

Anne is the face of the church extending her hand to those in need. And she wasn't looking for people to help. They came to her. She simply served the ones God placed in her path.

Every homeless person is a prodigal or a wounded traveler. *Each one* is our neighbor. The church, acting as a local congregation and in union with others, can offer the companionship and community the homeless need to help them elude the net of poverty. A lit candle can welcome them from darkness and show Christ's followers as the conveyors of God's true light.

CONCRETE WILDERNESS

Step on a crack and break a back.
Blind civilization marches on, marches over,
Those who have fallen through the crevices in our concrete world,
The small, the sick, the poor, the weak,
The wounded, the scarred, the scared, and the wandering,
Held captive under cold concrete.
Trudging over them, marching humanity chases vanity.
Our Redeemer defeats the jailer if we stop our march and see.

{Endnotes}

1   Anne Frank, *Goodreads*, accessed June 22, 2016, https://www.goodreads.com/quotes/198974-look-at-how-a-single-candle-can-both-defy-and.

2   1 Samuel 2:20; Matthew 26:6; 1 Corinthians 11:34.

3   Robert Frost, "The Death of the Hired Man," 1915, *Poetry Foundation*, https://www.poetryfoundation.org/poems/44261/the-death-of-the-hired-man.

4   Isaiah 58:5–7.

5   Jeremiah 1:7.

6   1 Corinthians 4:11–16.

7   Mark 2:1.

8   Luke 9:58; Matthew 8:20.

9   Christopher Weber and Geoff Mulvihill, "America's Homeless Population Rises for First Time in Years," *US News and World Report*, December 6, 2017, https://www.usnews.com/news/us/articles/2017-12-06/us-homeless-count-rises-pushed-by-crisis-on-the-west-coast.

10   *Social Solutions*, "2016's Shocking Homelessness Statistics," June 21, 2016, http://www.socialsolutions.com/blog/2016-homelessness-statistics.

11   David Smelson, "Homeless Veterans," US Department of Veterans Affairs, September 15, 2017, https://www.va.gov/homeless/nchav/research/population-based-research/mental-illness.asp; Substance Abuse and Mental Health Services Administration, "Homelessness and Housing," accessed February 27, 2018, https://www.samhsa.gov/homelessness-housing.

12   Recovery First, "The Homeless and Drug Addiction," August 24, 2011, https://www.recoveryfirst.org/blog/the-homeless-and-drug-addiction.

13   Billy Briggs, "Housing First: The 'Counterintuitive' Method for Solving Urban Homelessness," *The Guardian*, October 20, 2014, https://www.theguardian.com/cities/2014/oct/20/housing-first-the-counterintuitive-method-for-solving-urban-homelessness.

14   Noah Manskar, "NYC Homeless Population Is Growing, Research Shows," *New York City Patch*, December 7, 2017, https://patch.com/new-york/new-york-city/nyc-homeless-population-grew-4-year-data-show.

15   Covenant House, "Teen Homelessness Statistics," 2018, accessed February 27, 2018, https://www.covenanthouse.org/homeless-teen-issues/statistics.

Nineteen
CAREFULLY HANDLING
FRAGILE PIECES

"You are the light of the world. A city set on a hill cannot be hidden."

MATTHEW 5:14

*"Where there is no guidance, a people falls, but in
an abundance of counselors there is safety."*

PROVERBS 11:14 ESV

*"Glass is one of the most durable, yet fragile building materials.
While stained glass windows can last for centuries, as the great
cathedrals of Europe attest, they can be instantly destroyed by
vandals or by careless workmen. Extreme care must therefore
be exercised, even in the most minor work."[1]*

NEAL A. VOGEL AND ROLF ACHILLES

Like glass, people are durable yet fragile. Our bodies don't last for
centuries, but our souls do. Tending a soul requires great care. The

Master's hands are gentle yet resolute. Sometimes his shaping of us is hard to bear.

When I graduated from college, my job search began in earnest. I interviewed for a position selling life insurance and investments. The newspaper ad looked intriguing, but I was concerned that the hours would be mainly in the evenings, time I wasn't eager to put in with children at home. Yet I thought the interview went well, and I really needed a job.

The interviewer indicated that he was a single parent as well. A few days later, he called to say he didn't think this position was a good fit for me because of the evening hours. I agreed. Then he invited me to lunch. It was the first (and only) time I ever had an employment rejection turn into a date.

Lunch is a safe date. It was summer, and the children were out of school. If I thought it wasn't going well, I could claim I needed to get back to them. If he thought it wasn't going well, he could claim he needed to go back to the office. He picked me up on a sunny summer afternoon. We went to one of those not-cheap-but-not-expensive chain restaurants. I ordered a fruit platter. Our time together went well—until he dropped a bombshell. He wasn't *completely* divorced—just separated—and his wife did not understand him. I decided that if she couldn't figure him out, I probably shouldn't try. I didn't want to become the other woman in anyone's life.

Two close friends were proud of me. Cindy and I had met as young mothers whose children attended the same Christian school, and we had carpooled together. She was a pastor's wife who had been a pastor's child and a child of divorce. She gave me insight into what my children were dealing with. My other friend, Renee, is the gift of a big sister. She and I met in the church nursery. My two youngest were close in age to her two boys.

Both women had wisdom I didn't have. I trusted their advice and knew they had my family's best interests at heart. Miles ahead of me in their Christian walks, the two became companions to me, walking with me through my most difficult times. I leaned heavily on their counsel and still do. And they let me see their struggles too. They didn't let me idealize marriage and conjure up a fantasy of wedded bliss if I could only find the perfect prince. It wasn't that they showed me how bad marriage could be. They showed me how real it is—with highs and lows, happiness and hard work, very hard work. They did more than mentor me. They discipled me. They walked with me in their faith, showing me what it looks like to be fully reliant on God. To trust him in uncertainty and through challenges.

Being accountable to women who were discipling me made it difficult to rationalize an ill-advised relationship. They helped me stay on the narrow road that would protect my children and me from new trauma that could only cause new cracks, more shattering. They were proud of me for being able to spurn the advances of the interviewer. But he would not be my final temptation.

When my family's shattering was at its height, a friendship developed between me and Paul, the formerly homeless teenager who grew up to do weather reports for radio stations around the country, including the station where I worked. There was a window of several months when he was forecasting from Massachusetts for our station, and I was producing weather tapes for broadcast. We got to know each other as his first marriage was crumbling and as he was moving to a new job that still involved weather but no radio stations. Our work phone calls got longer. We exchanged home phone numbers. Then he traveled the five hundred plus miles to meet me. That was romantic and exciting. After nine years of struggle and separation, I thought he could be the one. My heart was all in.

But shortly after his visit, I put the brakes on. His divorce was pending. He was still married—just as the interviewer had been. I wouldn't be a catalyst to someone else's shattering, so we ceased communication. Despite appearances to the contrary, I knew that God might restore his marriage. And if he did, I didn't want to be a stumbling block to reconciliation. We would need to let God's will unfold in his time and not press for our own way in our own time.

So we waited.

I thought I would never see him again.

I went through the motions of life—work, church, parenthood, paying bills, cleaning house, doing laundry, and attending the children's activities. Cindy and Renee affirmed my decision. They both believed this separation was necessary. Their support reinforced what I knew within myself: Better to wait until the smoke clears than to build among fuming cinders.

I had married in idolatry the first time. This time I wanted to wait for God to show me his man, his way, and in his time. This better but difficult choice resulted from the painful shaping of circumstance and the soothing ointment of my friends' love.

Many churches today have focused ministries for single parents, but the biggest influences in our lives, mine and Paul's, were married people. God had set my friendships in place before I had become single again and my need for wise mentors became crucial. Cindy and Renee were intact pieces of glass showing me how to remain a stable piece within the window. That's what disciplers do best.

According to Ann Swindell, "discipleship means partnering with another Christian in order to help that person obey Jesus and grow in relationship with Him—so that he or she can then help others do the same." Discipleship is different from mentoring:

Mentoring has to do with what the mentor can offer to someone else through their own wisdom and experience; discipleship has to do with what Jesus can offer to someone else through His wisdom and presence.

While we are all called to become disciples of Jesus, we become disciples with one another, learning how to love God and each other as we go. We need to allow others to disciple us by letting them challenge us and encourage us in our walk with God.[2]

Learning how to love God works much the same way as love works in any other relationship. Love develops over time as two people find friendship and faithfulness in each other. People disappoint us; they aren't always faithful. We fail them sometimes too. Love deals with the messes disappointment and failure make in every relationship.

And sometimes, God seems to disappoint us too. But he's always faithful. He cannot fail. Loving God involves trusting him when our circumstances push us to question him. We learn to love him when we trust and watch him work.

At the same time, we disappoint God at times. He guides us back to him, if we let him. As God brings us through difficult circumstances, we learn we can trust him, even when life looks bleak, when relationships are stressed, when the roof leaks, when there isn't enough money.

Learning how to love others can be a lifelong effort. When the one we struggle to love seems unlovable, a loving God makes our effort fruitful. God's love for us, the unlovable, enables our love for others—lovable and otherwise. Disciplers help each other in that effort by modeling and encouraging love.

I watched life's circumstances draw Cindy and Renee deeper into their own faith, and so my faith went deeper. Cindy's family faced her husband's mysterious illness that sapped him of his energy and thrust her, for a time, into the role of primary breadwinner. Renee and her husband are retired. When their children were young, he went to work each day as a police officer about the same time most criminals did. She knew why he carried a weapon and wore body armor. She stood by as he witnessed the aftermath of unimaginable horrors.

Anne discipled me too. She modeled love in her care for the pregnant girls she housed and the homeless couple she helped. Their qualifications for her help were their need and her love. And, as disciplers do, she modeled deep faith when she quit a job that seemed perfect for her. God convicted her that the authority above her was not virtuous. She might have convinced herself to stay, but she obeyed God instead.

These women had busy, full lives, yet they invested in me.

Disciplers challenge us to go deeper in our faith. They urge us to rely on God when circumstances are confusing or when we don't see a way beyond them.

Disciplers will challenge us to move beyond our comfort zones to places where growth in Christ happens. If we look back over our lives, we might see a series of baby steps as we moved beyond silence to speech. Beyond anger to grace (I'm still working there). Beyond safety to risk. By our own will rather than chance circumstance, we choose obedience over the comfort of the familiar or the desirable. As we learn to leap in faith, we risk social standing, finances, or a journey to the unknown.

And disciplers encourage us. Before my divorce, I had been part of a married couples' class. Even though I attended church without a husband, I was still part of a couple. I dealt with the same issues others in the class faced. After the separation, I felt I had no place to go. There was a class called College and Career. It was filled with teenagers and early twenty-somethings. No one had a child; no one had been married. But one friend from the couples' class urged me to return. She persisted in inviting me back. By the time the church established a class for divorced people, I had returned to the couples' group. My situation had changed, but their love for me had not. Before my separation, the class had accepted me as a married person attending class alone. When I became single, they continued to accept me and disciple me.

Discipleship can be a short-term or long-term arrangement. My friendships with Cindy, Renee, and Anne have lasted decades. But some disciplers come and go. We take a class or work beside someone who gives us fresh insight into our Christian journey. We are different for having spent time with them. Then we move to a new season of life.

God is the Great Discipler. He guides our hearts as he did with Anne's in her job situation. He puts us in the paths of those who need us. He puts those we need in our path. He converges pathways. He chooses the times for the comings, goings, and crossings.

Companions and community holding me accountable helped me through eleven winters to a new season of life. They helped my family pick up our pieces. They showed us the window image a million different ways—in their own families, their own struggles, and their own faithfulness.

Eighteen months passed before Paul and I met again. Friends waited with us. And at the end of several more months, they celebrated two cracked pieces of glass becoming one.

Before he proposed, Paul asked Dad for his approval. We married in my father's small, stone, Presbyterian church. Cindy sang. Renee baked a formal tiered cake with a bride and groom topper. Anne baked some extra sheet cakes to accommodate our modest crowd of guests. When the pastor asked, "Who gives this woman?" Dad said, "I do, with my blessing." My community of fellow believers came together to rejoice, not just our wedding, but also the end of a season of shattering.

Is our story like Cinderella's and we lived happily ever after? No real story ever is.

Early in our marriage, we juggled jobs, kids' schedules, finances, and Paul's rotating shifts that required us to adapt to three different routines. We spoke different languages, each of us fluently. Paul spoke rural-stepdad. I spoke suburban-mom. My kids spoke suburban-teenager.

Paul's New England church had been small and legalistic. Our local church was larger and more relaxed without being lax. Sometimes he and I had conflict over how to manage kids and money. We struggled to understand everyone's language, wounds, and motivations. And through it all, we chose the intentional work of building accord.

Paul and I had much to learn about each other. Sometimes we still need a translator. The Master continues to gently and resolutely shape us. The light of the window is the Great Teacher.

Practice is the hardest part of learning, and
training is the essence of transformation.[3]

Ann Voskamp

{Endnotes}

1   Vogel and Achilles, "The Preservation and Repair."

2   Ann Swindell, "What Christians Get Wrong about Discipleship," *Relevant*, August 1, 2014, https://relevantmagazine.com/god/what-christians-get-wrong-about-discipleship.

3   Voskamp, *One Thousand Gifts*, 56.

twenty
STORIES IN GLASS

"Then I heard the voice of the Lord, saying, 'Whom shall I send, and who will go for Us?' Then I said, 'Here am I. Send me!'"

ISAIAH 6:8

"The Gothic stained glass style played the role of storyteller, offering Christian and secular scenes through intricate design and inspiring color and light. These windows shared the teachings of faith with all worshippers, whether literate or not. The clergy would use the windows to teach the gospel, ultimately elevating the art form as a symbol of the divine."[1]

ROBERT JAYSON

As pieces of glass, we never stop learning. And as glass in the window, we both learn and teach. Learning and teaching go hand in hand. And sometimes we learn and teach in a new place.

Except for a brief trip to Niagara Falls, Canada, I had never left the United States. By the time we married, Paul was already a seasoned globetrotter. As a meteorologist, he had worked on hot air balloon projects in Nepal, Saudi Arabia, and Japan. Early in our marriage, he went to Mexico for a week to work on a construction/outreach project. The team of several adults and teens constructed a small, adobe residence, typical of the kind inhabited by local families. The tools available to the team were what a mission organization *thought* were available to nationals in that location. But the organization was wrong. Instead of building relationships and expressing their love for the local people, the team did manual labor with shovels and hand tools. And they suffered the jeers of the locals who knew cement came more efficiently from trucks than wheelbarrows. More than once, a revolving cement truck drove past the team to another construction site where nationals were working without backbreaking toil.

Using resources within the community would have not only relieved the team of their backaches, it would also have provided more aid to the local citizens. And working *with* those citizens would have formed connections—the kind of connections that provide opportunities for mission workers to explain the God who sent them to do this arduous, sweaty work.

In this case, the sending mission organization fits a role similar to that of the US government running a welfare program. The mission team was working *for* others, not *with* them.[2] And in the process, their work didn't make the best use of available resources.

Robert D. Lupton points out that mission trips consume billions of dollars each year but "seldom yield appreciable improvement in the lives of those being served" and are often "large-scale misappropriations of charitable resources." For example:

> [American] mission teams that rushed to Honduras to help rebuild homes destroyed by hurricane Mitch spent on average $30,000 per home—homes locals could have built for $3,000 each. The money spent by one campus ministry to cover the costs of their Central American mission trip to repaint an orphanage would

have been sufficient to hire two local painters and two full-time teachers and purchase new uniforms for every student in the school.[3]

Lupton acknowledges the value such trips can have on those who embark on them, but he reminds us to empower those we serve rather than just doing something for them and going back to our lives, leaving them not much better off than they were when we got there.[4]

Paul's trip to Mexico was certainly a valuable experience for everyone on the team. They had an invigorating week, built connections within their team, and saw people living at a poverty level we seldom witness in our daily lives in America. They had made a home for a family and returned better equipped to minister at home. They had worked hard for one week to improve the lives of the people they helped. However, they also returned not having empowered anyone there and not having made any lasting connections that would enable them to continue speaking to the people they helped through the Christ they served.

A couple of summers ago, our church once again sent another team to build a house in Mexico. This trip was vastly different from the first one. This time, for months leading up to the journey, the mission team was a link between the church and the family who would receive the house. A ladies group made personalized quilts for the family. The congregation learned about the family members even before the team departed.

Once in Mexico, the team worked beside some of the locals. The mother whose house the team was building made meals for the workers. When the new home was completed, the team members stood in a circle and passed the front door key from hand to hand and finally to the hands of the woman who rejoiced in her new home. In turn, she went from one team member to another praying for each one. The family and the team spoke different languages, but her prayers moved the team to tears. Her life and her children's lives had improved. Connections had formed. Hearts had changed.

In late 2004, Paul and I decided to apply to go to Asia for our first mission trip together. We would travel to the same location in Asia twice. The first time, I was filled with eager anticipation. I knew there would be the discomfort of travel, the fatigue of jetlag, and—as a lifelong picky eater—the challenge of adjusting my palette to a new cuisine. God had been cultivating a passion in me for this culture throughout my life. My excitement kept fears of discomfort at bay.

Our journeys to Asia let us see not only how short-term commitment changes those on the mission team but also how the long-term commitment of a mission community (even if some of its members change over time) can make a lasting impression on those they serve.

I met "Sarah" in my first class when I was a novice EFL (English as a foreign language) teacher on a summer mission trip. From the start, she expressed interest in Christianity and had already done some investigating on her own. She had many questions, but one thing held her back. Her mother did not want her to become a Christian. Her mother said, "It doesn't matter what you believe. It only matters what you do." Sarah endured tremendous turmoil. Becoming a Christian would violate a principle Asian children learn at a young age: it is important, very important, to obey and please one's parents.

One morning I was going around the room, helping students with English pronunciation, when Sarah announced that she had a problem. She approached me and said, "Last night before I went to sleep, I heard a voice say, 'You must become a Christian before it is too late.' I do not know what the voice was."

Her statement shook me. I told her that I thought the voice was either God or an angel. She said that the incident was keeping her from concentrating on my lesson. I was stunned that she gave her summer camp English lesson that kind of consideration. She then sat down. Continuing the lesson, I determined to look for her at lunch, but she was nowhere to be found. I didn't see her for the rest of the day. Engaged in spiritual warfare, she isolated herself to wrestle with her inner torment.

The next morning, she entered the classroom and announced, "I am a Christian." She decided she simply would not tell her mother.

I decided to allow the Holy Spirit to deal with that. Yet I felt hostility toward Sarah's mother because she resisted Sarah's desire to become a Christian. I saw Sarah's mother as an enemy trying to divert her daughter from Christ.

A couple of months after we returned to the states, an email from Sarah astonished me. She had been growing in her faith but continued to keep her commitment to Christ from her mother. She read her Bible only when her mother wasn't home.

One day, her mother asked her an unusual question: "Who is the most important person in your life?"

Like any respectful teen from that culture, Sarah said, "You are."

Her mother said, "That is not the right answer. It should be Jesus."

While Sarah and I weren't looking, Christ had been working in her mother's heart.

My earlier sense that Sarah's mother was the "enemy" shamed me. I learned two important lessons. First, no person is ever the enemy. God desires all people to become his followers. Second, Sarah had to pay a price for her faith. She wasn't jailed, beaten, or killed, but, by embracing Christ, she may have been limiting her career possibilities, and she realized that "Now, I can't marry just anyone." In order to claim Christ, she had to defy her culture, not only because her government rejects him, but also because her upbringing required her to honor her mother by following her wishes. I had never before known anyone who went through such inward turmoil deciding to choose Christ. I had never before seen anyone count the cost.

One of our concerns about leaving Asia that year was Sarah's lack of a discipler. But her statement that she "can't marry just anyone" encouraged us that the Spirit was already leading her. One of the other teachers in her group introduced her to someone in an underground church. She would have Christian companions and community.

I had taught her some English. She, on the other hand, taught me about serious faith and the willingness to sacrifice. I also learned from the other teachers who worked with me. One young man taught me another important life lesson.

He knew his calling in life was not teaching, and he did not particularly enjoy the work he had before him that summer. One evening during an informal team gathering, he told me that he worked every day to keep his attitude positive—to resist the urge to count the days until he could go back to his more comfortable life at home. "I know God called me here to stretch me," he said.

He so clearly grasped a lesson I still struggle to embody. He worked hard not to complain—even silently. He worked hard to teach well. He was uncomfortable, but he did not struggle to release himself from his discomfort. He worked *against* yearning to go home. He worked through his discomfort to grow through it—to let God stretch him into a new shape, the shape of a more usable piece of glass.

Each person in our group brought varied talents and limitations to a team whose goal was to minister to people outside our team. Our overall goal was to show the light through the window to a dark land and minister to the people there, but in the process, God used us to sharpen each other and to build relationships within our team, with the nationals we worked with, and with our students. Some of those relationships continue today through email and social media.

In the big scheme of things, our trials were small. Over the course of our two trips, I didn't always like the food. We saw remarkable roaches, plentiful mosquitos, and a tarantula that I wouldn't have dreamed could move that fast. We suffered no great diseases, no threats to our safety. And our separation from loved ones was brief. The challenges and the discomforts that we faced pale in comparison to anything the famous gospel bearers of history confronted and that many persecuted believers around the world endure today.

The history of missions in Asia is awe-inspiring. In the fourteenth century, Catholic and Orthodox missionaries went to China. Catholic missionaries in China planted seeds that would bear fruit in Korea. In the nineteenth century, Protestants Adoniram Judson and William Carey went to Burma and India respectively.

Around the same time, Hudson Taylor founded the China Inland Mission. Taylor's missionaries learned the Chinese language and followed local clothing customs. These missionaries hoped to convert people to Christ, not to Western culture. They didn't equate acceptance of Western customs with a love for God as some of their contemporaries did.

At the beginning of the next century, the Boxer Rebellion in China claimed martyrs from Orthodox, Catholic, and evangelical traditions.[5] The Boxer Rebellion was a violent uprising against foreigners—business people and missionaries—between 1899 and 1901. Decades later, a local Chinese magistrate recruited British missionary Gladys Aylward to help the resident women in her area reject the cultural practice of foot binding. Later on, Aylward, at great risk to herself, refused to leave her adopted land during the Japanese occupation of World War II. She escaped the invasion and led more than a hundred orphans to safety.[6]

During the same period, Eric Liddell, Scottish missionary to China, also refused to leave his mission field in a Japanese prison camp during the war. In spite of a deal the Japanese occupiers had made with then British Prime Minister Winston Churchill, Liddell sent a pregnant woman to freedom in his place. He later died in the prison camp of a brain tumor.[7]

Great inspiration abides in the window of the past.

I came home from both Asia trips with the sense that I hadn't really done much. I had done no great work. God had *let me* watch *him* work. He showed me his work in our Asian friends and within our teaching community. He formed our connections.

One of the biggest lessons we learned came from seeing the change that occurred in the ministry there between the first trip and the second one. We shared our first experience with a retired couple who were veterans to the summer program at that school, but most on our team were rookie EFL teachers that year. During the second trip, the number of seasoned EFL teachers had grown. Several members were making their fourth or fifth excursion along with the two long-term veterans from our first trip.

Our trips to Asia represent a small piece of work by a small group of people with like-minded faith. We were all evangelicals. Had we gotten to know each other better, we may have found opportunity to find reasons for separation. But we focused on how to present Christ. We focused on our shared faith. We did not look at what made us different from each other.

When John Riccardo was a college student in Michigan, he and other young men participated in an evangelization effort. It was a local mission work. What makes that experience unusual is that Riccardo was Catholic and some of his fellow mission workers were evangelical Protestants. Catholics and Protestants came together in our most important mission—sharing the gospel. Today, John Riccardo is Father John Riccardo and a voice for accord.[8]

Relationships.

Companionship.

Community.

That is the church.

When we work in accord to share Christ, we get glimpses of God's work in people's lives. Through combined and sustained efforts, we gain even more: We see the effectiveness of the church as Christ prayed it would be.

As we engage in that work together, God continues to shine through the window his own work. Whether across the sea or in our own neighborhoods, we can offer the kind of support and encouragement my family got—the kind that Jesus uses to shape others and ourselves.

Expanding those relationships to include those of other faithful traditions enhances our community ministry, whether that community is local or abroad. Expanding those relationships expands the shaping work God does in us and in others.

Accord is following Christ in new relationships and in new seasons. The more usable we are, the more he can shine his Light to make new disciples, new pieces of glass to fit into the window. And as we go, we remember that he has promised to be "always with us."

You know plain enough there's somethin' beyond this world; the doors stand wide open. There's somethin' of us that must still live on; we've got to join both worlds together an' live in one but for the other.[9]

SARAH ORNE JEWETT

{ENDNOTES}

1   Robert Jayson, "Color and Light," Faith and Form, vol. 44, issue 1, accessed June 13, 2018, https://faithandform.com/feature/color-and-light.

2   Lupton, *Toxic Charity*, 35.

3   Ibid., 5–6.

4   Ibid., 69.

5   Father John, "Rebirth of the Orthodox Church in China: An Interview with Mitrophan Chin," *Journey to Orthodoxy*, May 13, 2013, http://journeytoorthodoxy.com/2013/05/rebirth-of-the-orthodox-church-in-china-an-interview-with-mitrophan-chin.

6   The Traveling Team, "History of Mission: Gladys Aylward," accessed July 30, 2016, http://www.thetravelingteam.org/articles/gladys-aylward.

7   Simon Burnton, "50 Stunning Olympic Moments: No8, Eric Liddell's 400 Metre Win, 1924," *The Guardian*, January 4, 2012, https://www.theguardian.com/sport/2012/jan/04/50-stunning-olympic-moments-eric-liddell.

8   *Common Ground: What Protestants and Catholics Can Learn from Each Other*, DVD, Kensington Production, 2006.

9   Sarah Orne Jewett, *The Foreigner*, August 1900, ed. Terry Heller, accessed November 24, 2014, http://www.public.coe.edu/~theller/soj/una/foreign.htm.

Epilogue
THE SHATTERED RESTORED

"Behold, I am the Lord, the God of all flesh;
is anything too difficult for Me?"

JEREMIAH 32:27

"I have become convinced that God thoroughly enjoys fixing
and saving things that are broken. That means that no matter how
hurt and defeated you feel, no matter how badly you have been damaged,
God can repair you. God can give anyone a second chance."[1]

MELODY CARLSON

Have you ever looked back on a season in your life and felt like it had all happened to someone else? In a way, it did. You have become someone new. The pain, the lessons, and all the calling out to God in the middle of the night changed you.

You look and sound much like the sand and colored glass you once were. But you now have small cracks where once there were open fissures. Your old friends recognize the cracks, but when you meet someone new, they can't even imagine how those cracks came to be.

My daughter Angela's rebellion—as most revolts do—ended through a series of circumstances rather than a singular turning point.

She and her boyfriend married. The arrival of their first child, Alex, and his battle with reflux stretched these new parents. Along their way, God filled cracks they carried from their youth.

And there is nothing like becoming a mother to help you want to reconnect with your own. As I was getting ready to leave her baby shower, Angela hugged me and hung on. Soon after, she called me at work. How did I make meatloaf? She wanted to know.

She called again. How could she get crayon markings off her mother-in-law's wallpaper—quickly? (In case you're wondering, toothpaste is the answer.)

Restoration had begun. We could work on leaving regrets behind.

Growing through rebellion and into adulthood, Angela became an objective outsider, the glue to help paste together all the broken pieces we had become. I have a picture of me with all five of my children at her wedding. Broken bits of glass standing next to each other, fitting together once more.

Today, Angela is a youth director at our church. A few years ago, the Easter service included the worship band playing John McMillan's "How He Loves" as various people from the congregation presented unspoken, cardboard testimonies. Cardboard testimonies celebrate the blessing of God repairing our brokenness. A series of people walked across the platform carrying cardboard signs representing challenges God had helped them overcome—child abuse, the loss of loved ones, teen pregnancy, marriage ills, and more. Holding our signs, Angela and I stood on the platform. Her sign said, "Rebellious Teen." My sign said, "Worried Mom. Prayed Every Day." The other side of her sign said, "By God's Grace, Leading Teens to Christ." The other side of mine said, "Proud Mom. God Answers Prayers." If my mother had still been alive, I could have walked across the platform twice. I had been a rebellious teen whose life God had transformed too.

At the end of the service, we were available to meet with parents worried about their own children. Time after time, we heard their amazement that Angela had once walked that path.

God's work in her life gives others hope that he can work in their own situations. A funny thing about transformation: people who do not witness it see only its results. They can't recognize how cracks have healed. They only see colorful, whole glass.

Personal faith, a supportive faith community, and devoted Christian companions nurtured Angela's small family as it grew. Three siblings followed the first child—two more boys and a girl. Today, that once fussy baby is married and an ordained associate/youth pastor. The couple has made me a great-grandmother to a wonderful little girl.

Aside from her youth director duties, Angela teaches drama at our local Christian school where Scott has taught since 1999. Their steady faithfulness to God, each other, their family, and their ministries helps heal and shape other pieces of glass for the window.

My son, Mike, is married to Carrie Jo, a medical technician in our local hospital's lab. They have a daughter and a son. As a child, Mike told his kindergarten teacher he wanted to be a railroader. The audience of parents at the graduation ceremony chuckled. The railroad was waning. Soon, they assumed, no one would work there. But today rail is alive and well and Mike is a railroader, a master electrician. The trains under his Christmas tree roll along still.

Trained in cosmetology, my daughter, Cyndi, has reentered the workforce after years as a stay-at-home mother. Her husband Andy is the other master electrician in our family. He played guitar at Mike's wedding while a friend of mine sang Harry Belafonte's "Turn Around" for my dance with the groom.

Cyndi and Andy have three sons, each birth its own adventure. These parents know that they too will "Turn Around" and find the years have passed like a breath.

Chris, my second son, is an accountant for a local paper mill. Tyne works for a local corporation. They recently adopted a baby girl and continue in faithful attendance at the Catholic church I attended as a child. We frequently discuss the differences and similarities between our traditions. Iron sharpens iron. Their faith encourages mine, and I trust mine does theirs.

My son, Rich, is a captain in the Army Reserves. He enlisted so close to the end of his college years that he did not reap any GI benefits toward his degree, but he wasn't looking for money. He wanted to become an officer. He wanted to lead. So far he has led other soldiers on two deployments. At home, he works at a thriving local enterprise as a software engineer and owns a house he shares with his dog, Boomer. Rich is the kind of man who picks up abandoned puppies he finds along the roadside and takes them to a safe place.

So, the children grew up.

How did restoration happen? Time and the Holy Spirit brought us together. Cracked glass, softened and smoothed.

There have been five weddings, ten grandchildren, and one great-grandchild—so far. We gather for birthdays and holidays and sometimes for no particular reason. Little by little, we craft new memories. Healing came. It still does.

Yet cracks remain in every heart. There is no unmarked glass in the image of the Bride. She is made of imperfect yet redeemed glass. Cracks can't help but show, but the light pours through anyway.

Our family accord is something I was not able to imagine two decades ago. Now, my dining room is full of family several times each year. I sometimes wonder if we had not endured our season of separation, whether we would be so deliberate about our gatherings. Would we value our time together as much as we do?

Sometimes there are empty places at the table. There are the challenges of jobs, sick children, and obstacles everyday life brings. Then, there are the not so everyday events. There were three deployments, one for Chris and two for Rich. The separation of miles makes a different kind of separation, the kind that draws hearts closer.

Several years ago, we revived a Thanksgiving custom from when the children were little. Each of us takes a turn listing three things we are thankful for. When we began this tradition anew, it had a flavor similar to when they were children, that of gentle teasing. But life has intervened with trials and joys. This yearly event is something each of us ponders before we gather. It gives us opportunity to pause and be truly grateful for our blessings—what we have, what we then lost, and what God may yet do for us. One year I marveled at their appreciation for each other, their hopes for each other's dreams, and their celebration of the journey of each other's lives. We are not a family that centers life just around Christmas and Easter.

Accord is a picture of the love of the sovereign God of absolute truth. We see him from different perspectives, different angles. Still he maintains his sovereignty, his absoluteness. He maintains the cracked glass in the window through which his light shines into the world.

In concert with him, we maintain our smallness and seek to honor him with our love for him—and for each other. As the church finds unity in him, the window of Christ and the bride becomes whole. It becomes a picture the whole world can see and understand. And it becomes the blessing of light God meant it to be.

And the congregation of those who believed
were of one heart and soul.

ACTS 4:32

EULOGEO

Eulogeo, the blessing, the story at the end,
But the story is never about the end;
It's about the beginning of the journey and the middle,
How we get to the end,
How we mend, elevate, and love each other.

Eulogeo is about navigating the path,
Following light and living truth.

Eulogeo.
May we be blessed to bless others,
And finish our path well.

{ENDNOTES}

1   Melody Carlson, *Damaged: A Violated Trust* (Colorado Springs: NavPress, 2011), 201.

Acknowledgements

Thanks are due the Christian Writers' Roundtable and the Altoona Writers' Guild for holding me accountable, critiquing my work, and encouraging me. To Bob Gresh for his support, advice, and encouragement; my brother Jeffrey Bulger for helping me with historical details; Mother Jacinta for her enthusiasm for the project and help in developing the chapter on mentoring; Suzy Weibel for telling me to write "because you're a writer;" and Cindy, Renee, and Anne for their love, support, presence of voice, and lives lived to shine Christ's light. You have been the angels over my right shoulder for many years.

W. Terry Whalin of Morgan James Publishing has offered consistent encouragement since the day we met at the Ohio Christian Writers Conference. And William D. Watkins—without his help, *Restoring the Shattered* would be so much less. Bill's insight and knowledge have refined grit into glass.

This book would never have happened without the loving support and assistance I got from Paul who spurred me on and read seemingly endless revisions. Special thanks are due to my children who have been my best teachers in life and who still inspire me daily.

Thanks to God for going before me, straightening my paths, and showing me his light through the beauty of the window.

About the Author

Writer and teacher **Nancy E. Head** was a single mother with five children under the age of fourteen when she attended Penn State University to earn a bachelor's degree in English and was elected to Phi Beta Kappa. Her career took a journalistic turn from radio news to newspaper reporting and then to education before she returned to the classroom to secure a master's degree in English from Indiana University of Pennsylvania.

Currently an instructor at Penn State Altoona and Great Commission Schools, she also spent two summers teaching English in Asia. She is a member of the Altoona Writers' Guild, the Christian Writers' Roundtable, the US Armed Forces Mothers, and Toastmasters.

When not teaching or writing, she restores antique quilts, crafts projects for her grandchildren, and helps her husband lead a small group at their church that is devoted to ministering to the needy in their community.

Printed in the USA
CPSIA information can be obtained
at www.ICGtesting.com
JSHW022326140824
68134JS00019B/1328